Writing

for

Success

PATRICIA O'REILLY

NEW
ISLAND

Writing for Success
First published 2006
by New Island
2 Brookside
Dundrum Road
Dublin 14
www.newisland.ie

ISBN 1 905494 14 9

Typeset by New Island
Cover design by New Island
Printed in the UK by CPD, Ebbw Vale, Wales

New Island received financial assistance from The Arts Council
(An Chomhairle Ealaíon), Dublin, Ireland

10 9 8 7 6 5 4 3 2 1

Patricia O'Reilly, a native of Dublin, lectures on various aspects of writing in UCD as part of the Adult Education Programme. She is the author of numerous books including: *Once upon a Summer, Time and Destiny, Earning Your Living from Home, Working Mothers* and *Felicity's Wedding*.

contents

ACKNOWLEDGEMENTS

Thank you to Roddy Doyle (novels), Anne Enright (short stories), Mary Kenny (journalism and non-fiction) and Siobhán Parkinson (writing for children), who willingly and generously shared their expertise.

And to Vincent Browne (*Village*), Ciaran Carty (*The Sunday Tribune*), Seamus Hosey (RTÉ), Brian Langan (The Liffey Press), Michael O'Brien (The O'Brien Press) and Sheila Wayman (*The Irish Times*), all of whose contributions were invaluable, as well as Jonathon Clifford on vanity publishing.

Also thanks to those authors and journalists whose words of wisdom on writing I borrowed: Jeffrey Archer, Maeve Binchy, John Banville, Stephen King, Dan Koeppel, John McGahern, Gillian Reynolds (*The Daily Telegraph*), J.K. Rowling, Di Speirs (BBC Radio 4) and William Trevor.

I'm also grateful to Jane Algar, Dublin City Public Libraries; the committee of Irish PEN; Peter McKimm, Irish Writers' Union; Mags Walsh, Children's Books Ireland; the staff of the National Union of Journalists (NUJ); and a special thanks to Richard Ryan.

Last but by no means least, I would like to acknowledge a special group of contributors. They are all the students with whom I've had the privilege of working in my capacity as lecturer and workshop convener in various aspects of writing. They are a constant source of education, inspiration and joy.

Introduction

Writing for Success is for anyone and everyone interested in writing. It's a widely quoted statistic that about a third of the population would like to write. Would-be writers come in all shapes, sizes and ages, and with a variety of aspirations: children scribbling what they blissfully believe to be the next Harry Potter phenomenon; teenagers studying journalism at third level, craving the excitement of scooping an international story; the factory worker dreaming of escape from the mundane; the opting-out executive pursuing a long-wished-for form of achievement; the unemployed person convinced they can make a new career; the person whose appetite has been whetted by selling a few pieces; the dedicated journal-keeper; and those who write for therapy.

If you fit into any of the above categories, you've picked up the right book. I hope you'll read it through, follow its guidelines and become the successful writer you want and deserve to be. Successful writing – and that translates into achieving your dreams – is what *Writing for Success* is all about.

All art is an inexact science and none more so than writing. The only exact point about writing is that there are no hard and fast rules to guarantee success. The theoretically unworkable often works in practice.

Whatever your reasons for choosing this book, I also hope it provides you with the key to the question I'm most frequently asked during my lectures, workshops and master classes: how can I get published?

As you'll discover when you read on, there aren't any mystical ingredients, no closely guarded publishing secrets. But there are certain practical steps you can take which provide the recipe for proficient writing, professional presentation and, hopefully, getting published.

You'll come across a wide variety of aids to help you to write, ranging from the sublime to the ridiculous. Should you so wish, you can enter the flow of writing with a self-hypnosis CD; learn how to write a book in 28 days, one hour a day, 100 per cent guaranteed; or be assured of publication under one of the many vanity imprints.

The facts and tips contained in *Writing for Success* are only the tip of the iceberg of the immense amount of information that's available on writing. But they are what I know, what I've done to get published and produced, and what I want to share with you.

1

getting started

'An inveterate and incurable itch for writing besets many.' Juvenal

INTRODUCTORY EXERCISES

The first exercise in this chapter is primarily addressed to those of you standing on the bank of the river, wanting to venture a toe into the swirling waters of writing but nervous of committing. You're not alone – there's a considerable population of you lining that bank.

We are often so busy wanting to have a life as a writer that we forget to have a life to write about. Before you read much further, put on a favourite a piece of music – for this exercise, soothing works better than heavy metal – and set aside fifteen minutes. Writing in longhand, describe a situation in your life that you are currently trying to metabolise. Here are a few key ideas, though if none of these appeal to you or if they aren't relevant, substitute one of your own:

- Coping with my boss's moods.
- My anger at my sister/brother/mother/father/best friend/lover/husband.
- Dealing with toddlers/teenagers.
- Living with my lover/husband/wife.
- Should I buy that Harley Davidson/mountain bike/skateboard/designer outfit?

Well done. You've crossed the first hurdle. And once you've made a start and got going, the subsequent chapters of *Writing for Success* are as relevant to you as they are to those who are already writing but who want to go a stage further by getting published or produced; the professional writers who dip into this book for information; and those recording for posterity, journaling or using writing as therapy.

WRITING REQUIREMENTS

Before setting sail on this writing voyage, it's heartening for the beginner to know that writing isn't misted in a blur of mystery. Most writing that is published or produced involves the acquisition of various skills as well as talent.

'Write what you like, then imbue it with life and make it unique by blending in your own personal knowledge of life, friendship, relationships, sex and work. Especially work,' advises American thriller writer Stephen King, one of the bestselling authors in the world, in *On Writing, A Memoir of the Craft*. He goes on to say that there is a difference between lecturing about what you know and using it to enrich the story. He considers enriching good but lecturing not. A case in point is lawyer John Grisham's legal stories, which are fiction but are solidly based in a reality he knows.

Like any other occupation, there are basic requirements for a career in writing, many of which are aided by an attitudinal approach that is consolidated by practice. While not making us perfect writers – perfection doesn't exist in writing – practice does take us along the road towards perfection. It also helps if you have:

- The mind of a detective – enquiring, keen, observant and thorough.
- A nose for a story.
- A smattering of psychology.
- A feeling for and empathy with people.
- A basic skill for storytelling.

The professional writer writes. 'Write,' advises Anne Enright, an internationally published, award-winning short story writer and novelist.

Most people who 'would love to be a writer' don't actually sit down and put any words on a page. They think 'being a writer' is like 'being thin', you get it just by wishing really, really hard.

Try not to hate what you write. Look at it. Write it again.

Confidence doesn't matter. No one who is any good has any confidence – why should you be any different? Put your lack of self-confidence in a box and leave it under the bed. Ten years later, when you open the box – it's gone.

Roddy Doyle's novel *Paddy Clarke Ha Ha Ha* won the Booker Prize in 1993 and achieved the distinction of selling more copies than any previous Booker winner. Doyle, who also writes non-fiction and scripts as well as children's books, endorses Enright's 'write' ethic:

I work all day, from about nine-thirty in the morning, sometimes earlier, until six in the evening. I work on several projects in any one day.

Writing is about discipline, as much as anything else. The writer must sit and write. This requires determination, a willingness to set aside time and work. Make the job easier at first by allowing yourself to accumulate pages. It's always good at first to be able to measure a day or an hour's work in pages or words.

There are many battles – what to write, and why, and how – but the first real battle is the willingness to find the time. I get tired of people telling me they'd love to write but they don't have the time.

I wrote *Paddy Clarke Ha Ha Ha* while teaching full-time and rearing a toddler and an infant and cleaning the kitchen and all the other excuses we use for not writing. Sometimes I only had twenty minutes, but the book became shaped by the little moments of time I could grab. One of the chapters is only two lines long. In a way, the conditions I was working under dictated the structure of the book. And it became a better book because of that.

'I'm always writing a novel, but never all day,' says Doyle. 'I can work on different projects as long as there is little in common between them. I could never, for example, write two novels at the same time. One project has to be a break from the other.'

Once you've got into the habit of writing on a regular basis, skill and technique are expertises which can and will be acquired and, when applied correctly, result in craftsmanship.

Hopefully, after serving the requisite apprenticeship, you'll graduate to those flashes of insight when you instinctively know how everything connects. It's known as 'thinking above the curve' and 'over-logic'. Whatever it is, it's magic.

WOULD-BE WRITERS

Would-be writers frequently fall into one of two categories:
- Full of ideas and images but wavering in a limbo of indecision about which writing route to take.
- An unquenchable drive to write but lacking ideas and feeling devoid of creativity and imagination.

Let's look at the full-of-ideas situation first. So you're bursting with all sorts of inspiration, characters, locations, bits of plots, etc., but can't decide what to do with them or which direction to go in. Should you opt for newspaper or magazine feature writing? Would you be better doing a non-fiction book? Or do you have moments of passion about writing that novel? Maybe you should go for short stories?

Only you can answer these questions. If you're in doubt about the direction of your writing, I suggest you keep an open mind at this stage. Spend time doing the exercises listed below and get into the habit of writing regularly to hone your skills. Eventually you will find the answers, and the relief of having a goal to aim for is enormous.

As for the second category of would-be writers, even when the drive to write is well and truly there – sometimes deep and silent within you, on other occasions positively clamouring for expression – you can still feel stymied by a lack of creativity or imagination.

Think back to what we said earlier about writing being a learned craft. Creativity and imagination are interlinked. Their function is to enable us to see and feel reality in a way we wouldn't otherwise experience. Imagination lights up reality. Imagination insists on reality. Despite what we may think, the function of the imagination is not just to escape into dreams; it can be creatively channelled and put to work.

To the two categories of would-be writers, it's facile to say 'just write'. But then again, that's about it. In the process, develop your own voice, and when you've done that, follow that voice, which is what Anne Enright did:

> I wrote one, unconventional short story, in a single draft and it was published in Faber's *Introductions to New Writers*. But before it was published, I spent two more years trying to write a 'proper' story and failing. A 'proper' short story was 'third person, past tense, with descriptive passages and plot points'. I really did try hard to do this, and I really did fail. It was only when I resigned myself to being completely useless as a writer that I sat down and wrote what I liked. Writing for me, requires a certain insouciance. Since then I have spent my time happily playing with voices.

RELEASING YOUR CREATIVITY

Look at the suggestions listed below, which are tried and tested methods of releasing creativity. For a start, choose the one that appeals most to you and give it eight to ten minutes of spontaneous writing. You'll be surprised at what you come up with. The next day, pick another heading and so on until you've completed all these exercises:
• Stream of consciousness.
• Trigger writing.
• Memoir.
• Dreams.
• News stories.

Stream of Consciousness

Get comfortable, close your eyes, blank your mind and allow in snatches of images/people/places. Using the 'blink' method, write what comes into your mind without thinking it through or going the route of wondering or analysing. Your 'blink' could range from a picture of a person to a particular location or an incident.

If the picture that comes into your head is of a person or a place, focus on impressions and sensations, using the five senses: sight, sound, touch, smell, taste. If it's an incident, get the bones of it down; you can fill in detail later. In each case, the important thing is to get the essence down on paper, be it in tumbling words, phrases, bullet points or sentences. Of course, it will need editing later, but you'll have a raw energy to work with.

The most famous example of stream of consciousness writing is James Joyce's *Ulysses*.

Trigger Writing

Trigger writing is a variation on stream of consciousness. Use a sentence, phrase or line of poetry that appeals to you and allow your imagination to take off. A sentence could run along the lines of a five-year old saying after swimming, 'I'm going to shiver myself warm.' In your mind, try to imagine who this child is. What does he or she look like? Where is the action taking place? Who is with him? How and why do they happen to be in that particular location?

A phrase could be as simple as 'prancing along the street with a high peacock tread'. Who is prancing? Why the prance? Or try the evocative 'long lilac-evenings'. What images does that conjure up? Who populates those evenings? What's the era and where's the location? What can happen on such occasions?

One of the most powerful examples of trigger writing is C.S. Lewis's classic series on Narnia. The story goes that one day during the Second World War, he came across some of the evacuees who were housed in his home. They were sitting around, bored, and he looked for a story to entertain them. One of the children had been interested in an old wardrobe in a bedroom and asked Lewis what was behind it. That simple question acted as a trigger for Lewis's creative spark. He began a tale about a family of children who had been evacuated to a large old house in the country which was owned by a mysterious professor. The story was never written down and eventually forgotten, but Lewis returned to the theme nearly a decade later when it formed the start of *The Chronicles of Narnia*, one of the best-loved and most successful series of children's books ever written. To date, the series has sold in the region of 80 million copies and has been successfully translated to the screen.

The possibilities are endless when you run with trigger writing. Again, write spontaneously, using the blink method.

Memoir

Like it or not, we are the sum total of our life experiences and we all bring a wealth of that to our writing. Try to write about your happiest or most profound childhood memory; your first day at school; or your most dominant memory. Most of us can remember our first kiss. Go back in time to that, recalling the sensations it evoked. By no means dismissing the light fiction of palpitating hearts and weak knees, one of the most powerful images of young sex has to be from Seamus Deane's *Reading in the Dark*: 'His tongue tasted odd – rough and smooth at the same time – like suede. She remembered thinking why would anyone want to. Especially as she knew that after such a long snog her pants would be wringing and they were navy schoolers.'

Dreams

For those who dream, treasure your dreams – they are a potent aid to writing. Have you ever awoken from a dream so powerful that you can almost taste it? Get it down on paper before its impact floats off into infinity, as dreams have a habit of doing. Keep a notebook and pen by your bed. And you know that wonderful feeling of floating between sleep and wakefulness? That can be an enormously creative experience. Capture the pearls of ideas contained in its essence before they float away, as, if not secured, float away they will.

News Stories

Newspapers and magazines are a fertile stomping ground for ideas, particularly if you think you're one of those people who don't have a great imagination. If you take to this method, perhaps you're destined for journalism. There are loads of newspapers (broadsheet and tabloid) and magazines (current affairs, fashion and style and trade) to choose from. Look at any publication of your choice, see what story draws you and do a 'what if' around it, looking at the various possible connotations.

GETTING DOWN TO IT

Talent alone won't make a writer, but it does help – indeed, it's a useful commodity in all walks of life. Success in writing, particularly writing you want to be paid for, depends largely on harnessing and directing your own talent, learning your craft, becoming adept at market analysis and having an awareness and commitment to satisfying market requirements as well as bucket-loads of dedication. Encouragement to stay dedicated can often come from an unexpected quarter, as Anne Enright knows:

> A woman came up to me outside Roches Stores in Henry Street in about 1998 and she said, 'I just love your work, I love everything that you write.' I had just abandoned my desk, in a state of complete despair. I found Ireland a very difficult place to write in, I was sure that I would not be able to make a dent, change anything, *proceed*. I have had critical success, and also won awards, but that stuff doesn't seem to be about your writing as much as about 'how the book is going' which is a different, more cynical kind of thing. So the woman outside Roches Stores was my street angel. A sentimental story, but true.

It's often said that within every Irish person there's a book just waiting to be written. Perhaps not a whole book, but many people certainly have some form of writing in them, waiting to escape. During the course of lecturing on various aspects of writing and convening workshops around the country, I never cease to be amazed at the amount of raw talent waiting to be channelled.

'Getting down to it' is the operative phrase in channeling that talent. No matter how talented a writer is or how great a story they have to tell, it has to be put down on paper and, that means putting one letter after another to make a word.

Enough words and you have a sentence, then a paragraph, a page and finally a completed piece. Then comes the editing, which separates the amateurs from the professionals. Editing, revision, writing and rewriting brings a piece of work up to publication/production standard. It's the lucky and rare writer that doesn't have to go through the editing process. As Anne Enright says, 'Every sentence has to earn its keep.'

Professional writers suggest that when starting out it's a good idea to write either for a set amount of time each day (even just ten minutes, which can be upped to fifteen after a few days) or to write a certain number of words – 200 is a good round number and it's only about a page of A-4, double spaced. It's optional whether you write in longhand or put it straight on screen. Go for whichever method is most convenient and comfortable for you.

Jeffrey Archer, author and English peer, has a work pattern that never varies when he's writing. He works from 6 a.m. to 8 a.m., takes a two-hour break for bath and breakfast, followed by another stint from 10 a.m. to noon. A run and lunch precede two more hours of writing between 2 p.m. and 4 p.m. After an interval for walking and thinking, his working day ends with another two hours of writing between 6 p.m. and 8 p.m. A huge hourglass, a present from his wife, dominates his desk and ensures he works the full 120 minutes of each session.

A word of warning here: making a coffee, ringing a friend or petting the dog is not writing. Baudelaire had the right idea when he said a writer's job was to put black words on white paper.

RUM

No matter what you're writing or about to write, think RUM: *relevant, understandable* and *memorable*.

Whether it's a feature or a short story, your piece needs to be *relevant* to the market (we'll take an in-depth look at market and market research later on). For instance, there's no point submitting a story with a love interest to a magazine which specialises in crime stories.

Anything you write, even a specialist piece, must be *understandable* to the readership you're aiming at. If you're an expert on broadband telephonics and are writing a feature for a national newspaper, it should be not only understandable but interesting to the ordinary man in the street. And there's no point in writing anything – be it a feature, short story, play, fiction or non-fiction book – which you don't consider to be *memorable*.

STRUCTURE

No matter how creative your writing is, in today's world, it works better if you have a structure. We'll look into this in more detail later on, but as a beginning strategy, keep the following in mind:

* Title: Should make an impact and whet curiosity.
* Opening sentence: At its best it's powerful, colourful, active and direct, and should be indicative of what follows. Remember: that first sentence is your introduction to your editor, publisher or producer as well as your reader or listener.
* Middle: The facts and happenings are in the middle of your piece, presented in such a way and with an amalgam of style and technique that they keep the interest of your reader or listener.
* Ending: Depending on your genre, endings can be a wrap-up, climax, continuance or acceptable surprise. Endings are important: they leave an aftertaste in your readers' and listeners' minds and hearts.

Later on we'll look at the ins and outs of fiction, non-fiction and the many and varied possibilities of feature writing, tailoring articles for newspapers and magazines which are published in both the North and South of Ireland, though first we'll take a preliminary look at the beginning, middle and ending of whatever you write.

Beginnings, Middles and Endings

Let's talk about managing your material. Nowadays the majority of pieces written for publication, with the exception of poetry or some examples of stream of consciousness prose, require a beginning, middle and ending. Poet Philip Larkin wrote of 'beginnings, muddles and endings'. He had a point, as frequently beginnings are grab-you-by-the-throat great and endings peak high, but middles can and do end up more of a muddle of facts, characters and incidents than the clarification they're supposed to be.

The layout triangle below is traditionally used as a means of sorting information. It helps to clarify material and to order thoughts before or even after writing your first draft.

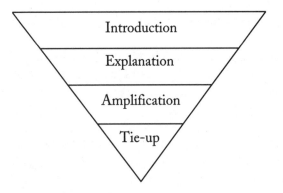

Beginnings

Openings are the most important part of anything you write. They are the first thing a publisher, editor or producer reads, and the first introduction of the reading or listening public to your work. They often consist of several paragraphs and can be a combination of two or more of the following:

- Distinctive incident opening: Snaps a 'word picture' at its most dramatic moment at the summit of interest.
- Quotation opening: Works well when using a familiar quote regarding the theme of the story.
- Short sentence opening: Can be a striking assertion used as a summary or statement of the most significant facts in the story.

- Question opening: Is similar to the short sentence opening, but used as an interrogation to challenge readers' knowledge or interest.
- Contrast opening: This presents two obviously different facts, emphasising the one that is the theme of the story.
- Analogy opening: Is similar to the contrast opening, but based on the similarity between well-known facts and the fact that is the story theme.
- Picture opening: Works as a graphic description of the story setting, as an introduction to the action or to the characters of the story.
- Janus opening: Looks back into the past or forward into the future for comparison with the present-day theme of the story.

Middle, or Body of Text

The rules of good writing particularly apply here. Be aware of CUE – *coherence, unity* and *emphasis.* The body of your text deserves thought and care in composition. Below are a few pointers:

- Use a central theme or main idea throughout.
- Eliminate extraneous material: edit, revise and rewrite.
- Smooth transitions from one paragraph to the next by avoiding abrupt changes of thought.
- Make paragraph beginnings forceful to impel the reader through the story.
- Use technical terms sparingly. Where appropriate, informal definitions should accompany them.
- Dress up dull or difficult patches with human interest items.
- With the exception of fiction, quote authorities to make the reader/listener feel that the facts are authentic.
- Weave the necessary background into the story for unity and coherence.

- Wherever possible, go for the specific rather than the general. Back up claims with facts or examples.
- Maintain a smooth, rhythmical variation in your writing to avoid monotony.

Endings

The endings or conclusions that work best follow the rules of narrative and expository writing. Again, they vary according to what you're writing.

- A condensed summary of the whole piece, i.e. briefly reviewing the salient facts, works well for magazine features.
- Climax or highest point of interest is particularly applicable to the short story.
- Flashback conclusion works as a restatement of the opening, rephrased in different language emphasising the important statements made at the beginning to round off the piece. Also known as bracketing.
- The new fact ending can be a cliffhanger in journalism, which generally incorporates a new fact that highlights the importance of your subject.
- A quotation ending works well with a relevant well-known quote, or quote from an interview or one of the characters.

THE ABCs OF WRITING

Despite all the advance preparation we may carry out, frequently good story ideas come at us literally from nowhere. Sailing out from the ether of the imagination, two apparently unrelated ideas fuse and, hey presto, you have a story. A writer must recognise and embrace these ideas when they show up and also be aware that although description has a habit of beginning in the writer's imagination, ideally it should finish in the reader's.

But good ideas are not enough – you must also be conscious of the ABCs of writing. For example, the 'four Ws' (why, when, where, what) and the 'one H' (how) is a mantra of journalism, but can also be usefully applied to most other forms of writing. Note the number of Irish writers, such as Maeve Binchy, John Connolly, Douglas Kennedy, Mary Kenny, Fintan O'Toole and Deirdre Purcell, who have successfully moved from journalism and feature writing to publishing fiction and non-fiction books.

The following is a list of some good writing rules:

- Accuracy: Watch out for misspellings – they give an impression of carelessness. In this era of computerised spell checks, there's no excuse for misspellings. Check and double check every name and spelling of it. Challenge every fact. If you fail to be accurate, you've fallen down in the most important fundamental of research.
- Brevity: Be brief, but not at the cost of completeness. Boil down your writing and eliminate waffle. Keep it compact. Avoid clichés.
- Clarity: Assume that if there's a possibility of the reader misunderstanding something, then he or she will, so be clear and keep your writing simple and straightforward.
- Coherence: Facts should follow facts logically. The story should stick together, not skip illogically from topic to topic and back again.

- Unity: A journalistic piece should deal with one topic. There will be many facts and ins and outs surrounding the story, but make sure it's still one story.
- Emphasis: It's best to put the most important facts first, particularly in journalism. Put the other facts in decreasing order of importance. That way, readers know that what they've just read is more important than what's to come.
- Objectivity: Try to keep aloof where it's necessary to write objectively. Don't use emotive phrases. Detachment helps you to present an impersonal, unbiased and unprejudiced story.

2

print journalism: newspaper and magazine features

'When a dog bites a man that is not news, but when a man bites a dog that is news.' *New York Sun*

'Journalism is ephemeral and I don't think it lasts. It is said to be "writing on water". I have forty years of cuttings, but I am not sure any of it is particularly memorable,' says journalist Mary Kenny, who is firmly established on both sides of the Irish Sea as a writer and journalist contributing to over twenty publications, including the *Irish Independent, The Times,* the *Guardian, Daily Mail, Spectator,* and the *Irish Catholic* and *Catholic Herald.* She has also written several non-fiction books and a play.

> If someone asks for an opera libretto, the professional writer should be able to respond: 'When is the deadline?' (Or, perhaps, in the American wisecrack: 'Do you want it Tuesday, or do you want it good?'). Keith Waterhouse, a veteran of the journalism trade, once said that a journalist is basically a professional writer; and a professional writer should be able to turn his, or her, hand to anything.

There are roughly 1,000 print publications throughout the North and South of Ireland. These vary from national broadsheet and tabloid newspapers, through provincial and local, to glossy and trade magazines and in-house news sheets, not to mention book publishers. With the likely exception of in-house publications, the majority of publications not only use freelance writers, but are actively interested in finding new voices and fresh, innovative ideas. Indeed, ideas are the keystone of a freelancer's repertoire.

The main area of opportunity for freelance writers in journalism is in features, an extraordinarily broad brief which can consist of:

- Human interest, including profiles.
- News.
- Seasonal.
- Travel.
- Expert, such as fine arts, cookery, gardening, etc.
- Advertising.
- Reviewing (art, books, theatre, concerts and gigs, movies).

Human Interest

Human interest stories touch the chords of our hearts and are a keynote focus of tabloid newspapers, whose sales are constantly rising, primarily because of their subject matter and the readability of their contents. We've all paused, read and identified with the human devastation of New Orleans after Hurricane Katrina, the story of the hole-in-the-heart baby, the Mother of the Year contest or the boy who rescued his pal from drowning.

Equally, we're fascinated by the stories of the real people behind the news, the private person lurking behind their public persona. Profiles never go out of fashion and a good profile writer will always be in demand. Deirdre Purcell's in-depth profiles each week in the *Sunday Tribune* made her a household name long before the publication of her first bestselling novel.

News

News features are tied into and closely allied to the hard news stories of the moment. Many readily take on the mantle of human interest. For instance, the 2004 St Stephen's Day tsunami started as a hard news story, then evolved to news features and human interest pieces. More than a year later, it's still providing copy. Equally, a factory closure in Cork or Belfast will be covered in a news story with detailed facts, such as the number of job losses, income lost to the area and the overall effect on the economy. A news feature can take that further by, say, interviewing a family whose breadwinner has lost his or her job and finding out what it means to that family in terms of mortgage repayments, schooling, lifestyle and so on. Through nosing around the peripheries of a hard news piece, an aspiring journalist who is attuned to and informed of a given situation can come up with many saleable stories.

Seasonal

Who hasn't thrown their hands up in disgust at the end of September, just when the back-to-school features have finished, at the countdown to Christmas? Christmas, Easter, summer holidays, schooling, exam stress, sales, Halloween and Valentine's Day are all grist to the mill of freelance writers' lives. Think of the options and variety of angles on which you can write about Christmas – shopping, food, presents, parties with a difference, cooking, family organisation, hangover cures, house decoration, not forgetting self-glamming.

With 'seasonals' you have to get your proposal in on time. If targeting newspapers, you can pitch your idea about six weeks in advance, whereas for monthly magazines, which go to press some twelve weeks before being available in the bookshops, think four or five months ahead.

Travel

There is a continuous market for travel. Look in any of the daily or Sunday newspapers or magazines and you'll invariably see a travel piece. For specialist writers into fishing, for example, the focus can be on a location that has good fishing, including the quirks, pluses and minuses. The trick is to capture the essence of a place and then to run sidebars on how to get there, accommodation, 'not to be missed' lists, etc. Sidebars are columns with bold type used in journalism to convey facts/statistics, usually positioned as one column down the side of text, hence the name.

Expert

Experts occupy a special niche in the world of newspapers and magazines. More often than not, experts are passionate about their subject, and, as we've previously said, passion is a great blessing for all forms of writing. It's mainly a matter of sourcing the right outlet, approaching the feature editor and making your pitch, all of which we will be going into later.

Advertising

These features, sometimes billed as special reports or commercial features, are an important source of revenue for newspapers and magazines. To succeed in this discipline requires the acquired skill of being able to realistically balance journalistic integrity with drawing in advertising revenue.

Reviewing

Reviewing is closely allied to the expert category. A passion and a knowledge of, say, movies, music gigs, concerts, books or the theatre will ensure that you pick up reviewing work easier than someone who is indifferent to and uninterested in the subjects. Follow the style of the publication you're reviewing for and make sure to get titles and names right.

GETTING IDEAS

'Writing is a dog's life, but the only one worth living,' Gustave Flaubert

So from where do you get your ideas for features? From everywhere and anywhere. Mary Kenny's ideas come from:

> Talking to people, going places, seeing movies and plays, having experiences, keeping a notebook in which I jot down thoughts which may link up with a topic that becomes topical.
>
> For example, on an exceptionally cold day in January, I jotted down: 'fur coat – ten reasons why you should wear one, in defiance of anti-fur protesters'. And reviewing a story about Elton John's 'wedding', I thought of an ancestor of my husband, a Victorian homosexual who entered into a heterosexual marriage because of the social values of the times. He was often unhappy, yet was adored by his children, and now has over 80 descendents, all interesting people. An outline for a piece with a slightly different take on gay unions.

You have an idea. It's a brand new angle on, say, child-minding. 'New angle' is the important phrase here because childminding is a subject that has received considerable media coverage, and hackneyed stories don't work in today's press.

The Childminder's Story

A childminder from Poland believes her human rights are being violated by the family whose children she is caring for. She's willing to go on record. Will her story stand alone? Or should you get other back-up interviews, such as a mother employing another Polish child minder, the relevant association/s for childminders, an association for non-nationals? And how about some vox pops from working mothers? (Vox pops comes from the Latin and literally means 'voice of the people'. They are short quotes on the relevant subject from a cross-section of related people.)

It makes sense to set out your planned feature along the lines of the following diagram.

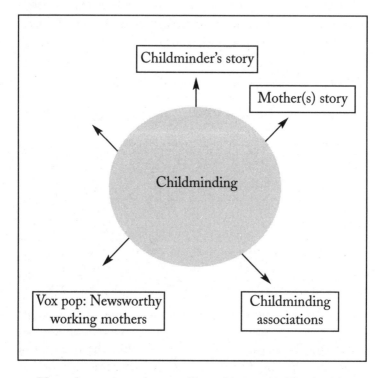

How do you go about selling this story? Firstly, it's an interesting subject, one which concerns a large percentage of the population. Good.

Secondly, ensure that your chosen subject not only holds your interest, but grabs you. If it doesn't, chances are it won't grab the commissioning editor and go on to spellbind the publication's readers. When we're passionate about a story, we pitch harder, research better and write from the heart.

Childminding fits all the necessary criteria. It isn't a brand new story, but you have this original angle.

The next step is to offer the idea to a suitable publication. There's no point approaching, say, a golfing magazine with a piece on childminding, unless – and this is important, as it applies to any specialist magazine – it can be tweaked to fit in. This is the stage where you do some all-important market research. The importance of market research will come up again and again throughout this book, but basically what's required for journalism is little more than common sense along with acquiring a feel for the print market.

The most efficient way to do market research is to buy a bundle of newspapers and magazines, sit down with a coffee and analyse their contents, paying special attention to both editorial content and advertising. For those of you interested in breaking into journalism, remember: newspapers and magazines wouldn't exist without their quota of writers.

Jennifer Stevens, editor of *Irish Tatler*, an upmarket monthly primarily aimed at women in their twenties to thirties, encourages newcomers to journalism and welcomes unsolicited pitches by e-mail, which, she says, should be followed up about a week later by a phone call. 'Journalism is a competitive business and people who want to break into it must be willing to follow through. We're more likely to commission further pieces if we receive grammatically correct, clean copy without spelling errors.' *IT*, like the majority of magazines, accepts features as a Word attachment as well as copied into the body of the submitting e-mail.

Sending out unsolicited manuscripts is regarded as unprofessional and isn't recommended. Indeed, *Woman's Way* has a paragraph on its contents page stating that it doesn't accept unsolicited material. While the general consensus among commissioning editors is that they welcome professional newcomers, they shudder at enthusiastic amateurs who are ignorant of the protocol of the business.

Getting back to our example, you've taken the first step, done your market research and settled on approaching one of the dailies with your childminding story. It's a good choice – Irish dailies have proven records in cutting-edge features.

The situation becomes slightly catch-22 at this stage. Your piece involves several interviews. Should you approach those people before or after talking to the commissioning editor?

As a beginner, it's probably best if you make a preliminary approach to your interviewees, saying something along the lines that you're hoping to sell this idea to such-and-such a paper and when – not if – you get the go-ahead, ask if they would be willing to be interviewed. Usually they agree. The general public is wonderfully generous interviewee material.

The second step involves making a phone call that will arm you with the name and e-mail address of the features or commissioning editor. The majority of commissioning editors favour an e-mail pitch rather than a telephone sell. Back at your desk, compose your e-mail, remembering that this is the vehicle that will sell your story.

In the subject box, write something along the lines of Childminding – Proposed Feature. Keep the opening paragraph brief and pithy – it needs to whet the editor's appetite and, if possible, particularly if you're new to feature writing, prove that you have the credentials to write on this subject: perhaps you've worked as a childminder or employed child-minders? Or maybe you just have your Polish childminder's story – this is the weakest approach.

Include your proposal in the body of your e-mail – an attachment may not be opened. It should clearly state who you propose to interview and their relevance to the piece. It's professional to suggest the approximate length of your piece, having previously checked the favoured word count of that particular publication for your style of story.

An easy way to estimate word count is to count the words in, say, five lines in one column of print, for example, fifty-five words, i.e. eleven words per line. Now count the number of lines in the feature and multiply the number of lines by words. A popular feature word count for broadsheets is around 800 to 1,000 words; tabloids can be as low as 250 words, while magazines can run from 2,500 to upwards of 5,000 words.

After sending the e-mail, follow up with a phone call a week later. In the event of being put through to the commissioning editor, your question is simple: are they interested in freelance contributions? Invariably the answer will be yes – no editor wants to miss out on a scoop.

Now is when you have to sell your idea – and indeed, yourself – succinctly and with enthusiasm. Have your facts exact and precise so that you can make a concise pitch – it's enormously beneficial to have this written down in advance – and remember to talk slowly. Slow speech carries more weight and has a certain gravitas of expertise.

To be asked for 'sight' of a completed story at this stage is a definite cause for optimism. Get your piece in as soon as possible. Journalism has an immediacy about it that requires instant responses.

The fact that an editor has expressed interest calls for knuckling down, researching, writing and polishing. Leave the celebrations until it's accepted, or even better, until you've received payment. Exciting as it may be to have your piece accepted, do follow the checklist of guidelines from the National Union of Journalists listed further on.

The more likely scenario, though, is that if the features editor is interested in your idea, you'll be asked to present your proposal in writing, particularly if you're a newcomer to the publication. Respond immediately by e-mail with amplified bullet points. To make your initial pitch you'd have had to have all the relevant information at your fingertips, so there's no excuse for delay and a prompt response is seen as professional.

If you haven't heard back a few days after you've submitted your proposal:

- Check by telephone or e-mail that it has been received.
- Ask if further information is required.
- Enquire when you'll know if your idea has been accepted.

If the answer to the latter is something along the lines of 'probably Thursday afternoon, we'll let you know', then reply, 'not to worry, I'll ring you.' Make a note of it in your diary and follow up. Invariably, editors are overworked, and it's not that they don't bother making that call to you, but often they don't have or make the time. It's better to become aware sooner rather than later that one of the requisites of being a writer – any kind of writer – is acquiring hard neck.

So it's Thursday afternoon. Make the call around 3 p.m. – back from lunch but not yet time to think of going home – and get the go-ahead. Congratulations. You have now been commissioned.

THE COMMISSION

A commission is a contract in law. It's common business practice to agree terms and to confirm in writing prior to delivering your copy.

According to the National Union of Journalists (NUJ) guidelines, at this stage the editor should let you know:
- Adequate specification of material to be published.
- Likely date of publication.
- Required length of written material.
- Rate of payment.
- Arrangements for reimbursement of expenses.

This checklist is seldom clear, so if in doubt about any of the points, it's up to you to clarify them.
- Content: A detailed specification of what is to be included in the story.
- Length: Keep in mind that for every 100 words of journalism, you have ten to play around with.
- Deadline: If your deadline is 11 a.m. on Tuesday, have your piece in by 10.30 a.m. at the latest.
- Ask about the anticipated publication date.
- Confirm that you'll get a by-line – having your name under your story is much of what writing is about.
- And last but by no means least, do raise the subject of payment and expenses.

While a word-of-mouth contract is legally binding, wherever possible, even though it's no longer commonplace practice, verbal agreements should be confirmed separately from your submission in writing. This can be done by e-mail, fax or letter.

Check how the editor wants the copy. Most newspapers and magazines expect copy to be sent by e-mail.

If e-mailing your story, put 'Childminding' in the Subject box, confirm your telephone conversation and send the piece as a Word attachment. At the top of your first page put the catchword (in this case 'Childminding'), your name and the date (month/day/year). Example:

Childminding   Anne O'Shea   September 20 2006

At the end of piece, include your address and phone numbers, as well as a word count and ©, the copyright sign. The copyright sign can be accessed by bringing your cursor to the relevant place in your text, clicking Insert at the top of your screen, then Symbol, then clicking ©, Insert and Close.

Not many editors favour postal submission these days, but those who do expect them to be well presented, neatly typed and correctly spelled.
- Use A-4 white paper – laser quality is fine.
- Head up the first page (frontispiece) with the title; your name, address, telephone numbers, e-mail address and fax number; word count; copyright symbol (©); and date (month/day/year).
- In the header of subsequent pages, include the file name, page number, your name and date.
- Allow generous margins (approximately 4 mm).
- Print on one side of the page only.
- Use Times New Roman, font size 12.
- Use double-spaced line spacing. Indent three spaces for each new paragraph.
- Do not carry incomplete paragraphs over the page.
- Write 'more' or 'm/f' at end of each page.
- At the end of the last page, write 'ends' and give word count.
- Enclose a self-addressed envelope (SAE) for return.

Example of a frontispiece:

Childminding

By
Anne O'Shea

Words: 850
© aos/9/2006

13 Grove Road,
Kilkenny
Tel: 056 7743229
Mob: 087 6772834

'The most important quality for a journalist is *curiosity*,' says Mary Kenny. 'What makes people tick? What is the story behind the story? The rest can be learned. A journalist doesn't need to be a beautiful writer, just a clear and competent one: beautiful writers may be frustrated by journalism, in the end.'

GUIDE TO PAYMENT

The NUJ has a code of minimum guidelines of payments. Due to various contretemps, there have been no negotiations between newspapers and the NUJ, so for the past number of years the Irish freelance fee structure has remained static.

For instance, for a 1,000-word feature, the *Sunday Business Post* pays €227.92, while Jemma Publications, which has a stable of commercial and business magazines, rows in at €119.36. The *Irish Independent* and *Sunday Independent* pay €108.94 for 900 words and the NUJ rate for the same wordage in *The Irish Times* is €113.12 (see below for *The Irish Times* rate of payment).

Despite the majority of newspapers being unionised, negotiation is always an option, though it's a good idea to wait until you've proven your ability before making demands. The majority of commissioning editors are fair-minded about payment. Most magazines published in Ireland aren't unionised and their fee structure varies to take into consideration the writer's public profile and input into contents.

Politicians love the expression 'living wage', though when applied to freelances that simply means fair payment for work done. If you spent a total of eight hours researching, interviewing, writing and polishing your piece, then at the very least you should be paid the minimum daily national wage, plus any expenses you may have incurred. (A note here about expenses: you cannot expect a newspaper or magazine to pay for taxis, bottles of champagne or meals at high-priced restaurants, but public transport, mileage and the occasional coffee or round of drinks are usually acceptable. Make sure to keep all tickets and receipts.)

Most established publications have set days in the month for paying contributors. A quick call to the person dealing with contributors' payments will sort that out and you should receive a cheque within four or five days of the payment date. Unless payment runs way behind or becomes problematic, it's not something your editor needs to be involved in.

IF AT FIRST YOU DON'T SUCCEED...

Now let's look at the less successful scenario when the commissioning editor turns down your piece. More often than not, this will be done without giving you a reason. Don't lose heart. The current ratio on the freelance market for commissioning is around 1:7. In other words, as a newcomer to the business, you may have to pitch seven times before a piece is taken up.

If you're still interested in doing work for that publication, ask if you may submit further ideas. If your submission/piece has been presented in a professional manner and is up to the standard of the publication – and make sure it is – you'll likely receive an affirmative reply.

Do go ahead and offer other ideas (no more than three at any one time). When starting out, a well-known freelance journalist was invited to submit ideas, and in her own words 'burnt the midnight oil' to come up with fifty ideas and treatments, ten of which paid off. Persistence matched to professionalism has a habit of paying off in journalism – indeed, in all forms of writing. E-mail your ideas and put a note at the end of your submission that you'll phone on a specific date and time, about four days later, and follow that through.

Having done your market research, there's nothing to stop you sending out multiple feelers. The same subject may work equally well for the *Belfast Telegraph* and *The Irish Times* as for the *Daily Star*, but the treatments and approaches for broadsheets and tabloids are different, as you'll note from studying the newspapers.

If you get an acceptance from one newspaper and you've pitched the same idea to another publication, make sure to inform the second immediately. Do be aware that newspapers and magazines editors prefer exclusivity of approach, but as a freelance new to the market, you need to be able to operate with several balls in the air. After proving your professionalism over time with the publication/s of your choice, it's quite likely that you'll be offered a permanent slot, or even asked to join the staff, which is Mary Kenny's preferred route for a journalist starting out:

> The traditional advice was 'work on a local paper', and I think this may still be the best. The regional press in Ireland is very good, in my opinion, and has a real sense of the community around it. I wouldn't ever start by going freelance, as you need to work on contacts and connections, and that is best done by having a job. After a few years in general journalism, it's a good idea to develop a speciality. Sports and business are two very sought-after specialisations. General features the most over-crowded.

The Irish Times features editor, Sheila Wayman, says, 'While we can use only a limited amount of material from freelance contributors, our features department welcomes proposals, particularly for articles on a specialisation not covered by our staff, strong human interest stories, features with a news angle or an unusual angle and on new lifestyle trends.' She says suggestions are best sent by e-mail to the features department (features@irish-times.ie), marked for the attention of the features editor (Sheila Wayman), the editor of the Saturday magazine (Patsey Murphy) or the arts editor (Deirdre Falvey), with a snappy outline of the idea.

'If you haven't heard back within a week, a follow-up e-mail or phone call is welcome, as e-mails can get overlooked in the huge volume of material sent in. Once the idea is approved, first-time contributors would be asked to submit the article without being guaranteed publication.'

Payment for features accepted by *The Irish Times* starts at €200 for 1,000 words, but the fee will be adjusted to reflect the amount of work the article involved. Standard features range in length from 800 to 1,600 words.

Equally, Gail Walker, features editor of the *Belfast Telegraph*, is happy to receive e-mail pitches with ideas for features.

The focus of weekly current affairs magazine *Village*, edited by Vincent Browne, is hard news stories, though he notes 'we take few freelance contributions because of budget constraints.' Again, he favours an e-mail approach, and while the inclusion of a CV by an unknown writer may have significance, Browne says, 'The main issue is the quality of the article and its relevance.' While the magazine doesn't commission features from unknown writers on pitch, 'we would encourage, on occasion, "unknowns" to write a piece and let us see it and we do support new journalistic voices.' Browne also advises those wanting to break into journalism to 'do hard news stories on issues that matter and write them carefully, without opinion, getting to the central point in the first clause.'

While feature writing is a happy place to be in the pecking order of journalism, having your own column is the ultimate. 'I consider it a privilege to have a column, and also a responsibility,' says Mary Kenny.

> It is rewarding to get feed-back from readers who sort of get to know you. But there are many more columns today than there used to be, and that makes it more competitive too. You really do need to have something to say to produce a regular column: however casual and off-the-cuff it looks, there should be real thinking and working behind the composition. Yeats said something similar about poetry: it should read as though it is effortless, but in truth it should be composed by the sweat of the brow.
>
> And yet, the kind of journalism I most admire is good reportage. It is marvellous to come across, especially in old newspapers, well-observed and accurate coverage. There was some fabulous reporting of Parnell's funeral, with reporters noting exactly what the floral tributes strewn on his grave said. The GAA's read, 'We will avenge'! These are the details of the journalism of record which become, afterwards, the stuff of history.

NEWSPAPERS

Below is a list of national and some of the provincial and local newspapers in alphabetical order. If you plan to approach a particular publication with an idea for writing a feature piece, familiarise yourself with the newspaper, its editorial content, house style, layout and type of advertising. At the risk of repetition, market research is all important.

Belfast Telegraph

Interested in features relating to Northern Ireland. Payment by negotiation. Editor: Martin Lindsay. Features editor: Gail Walker. 124-144 Royal Avenue, Belfast BT1 1EB. Tel: 028 9026 4000; fax: 028 9033 1332; e-mail: editor@belfasttelegraph.co.uk; website: www.belfasttelegraph.co.uk.

Evening Echo (Cork)

Features and news for the area. Editor: Maurice Gubbins. 1-6 Academy Street, Cork. Tel: 021 427 2722; fax: 021 480 2135; e-mail: maurice.gubbins@eecho.ie; website: www.eveningecho.ie.

Evening Herald

General and specialist features. Payment by arrangement. Acting editor: Stephen Rae; features editor: David Diebold. Independent House, 27-32 Talbot Street, Dublin 1. Tel: 01 705 5333; fax 01 872 0304 e-mail: hnews@unison.independent.ie; website: www.unison.ie.

Ireland on Sunday

Mid-market tabloid. Welcomes unsolicited material. Up to 2,500 words for features. Payment by negotiation. Editor: Paul Drury. Embassy House, Ballsbridge, Dublin 4. Tel: 01 637 5800; fax: 01 637 5880; e-mail: news@irelandonsunday.com; website: www.irelandonsunday.com.

Irish Daily Mail

Relevant features and news items, approach by e-mail. Payment by negotiation. Editor: Paul Drury. 3rd Floor,

Embassy House, Herbert Park Lane, Ballsbridge, Dublin 4. Tel: 01 637 5800; e-mail: news@dailymail.ie.

Irish Daily Star

As well as features, general articles relating to news and sport. Length 1,000 words. Payment by negotiation. Editor: Gerard Colleran; news editor: Michael O'Kane; sports editor: Eoin Brannigan. Star House, 62A Terenure Road, Dublin 6. Tel: 01 490 1228; fax: 01 490 2193; e-mail: features@thestar.ie; website: www.thestar.ie.

Irish Examiner

Feature material mostly commissioned. Length 1,000 words. Payment by arrangement. Editor: Tim Vaughan; features editor: Joe Dermody. 1-6 Academy Street, Cork. Tel: 021 427 2722; fax: 021 427 5477; e-mail: features@examiner.ie; website: www.examiner.ie.

Irish Independent

Special features on topical or general subject. Length: 700-1,000 words. Payment: editor's estimate of value. Editor: Gerry O'Regan. Features editor: Peter Carvosso. Independent House, 27-32 Talbot Street, Dublin 1. Tel: 01 705 5333; fax: 01 872 0304; e-mail: inews@unison.independent.ie; website: www.unison.ie

The Irish News

Features of historical and topical interest. Editor: Noel Doran, n.doran@irishnews.com; features editor: Joanna Braniff, features@irishnews.com. 113-117 Donegall Street, Belfast BT1 2GE. Tel: 028 9032 2226; fax: 028 9033 7505; website: www.irishnews.com.

The Irish Times

Specialist contributions (800-1,600 words) by commission on basis of idea/s. Payment at editor's evaluation. Editor: Geraldine Kennedy. Submit ideas by e-mail marked for the attention of the features editor (Sheila Wayman); the editor of the Saturday magazine (Patsey Murphy) or the arts editor (Deirdre Falvey), with outline of idea. 11-15 D'Olier Street, Dublin 2. Tel: 01 679 2022; fax: 01 671 9407; e-mail: features@irish-times.ie; website: www.ireland.com.

News Letter

Special features. Payment at editor's valuation. Editor: Austin Hunter. Century Newspapers, 46-56 Boucher Crescent, Boucher Road, Belfast BT12 6QY. Tel: 028 9068 0000; fax: 028 9066 4412; website: www.newsletter.co.uk.

Sunday Independent

Special features, length according to subject. Payment at editor's valuation. Editor: Aengus Fanning; deputy editor – features: Anne Harris. Independent House, 27-32 Talbot Street, Dublin 1. Tel: 01 705 5333; fax: 01 872 0304; e-mail: snews@unison.independent.ie; website: www.unison.ie.

Sunday Life

Features of interest to Northern Ireland tabloid readers. Payment by arrangement. Editor: Martin Lindsay; features editor: Audrey Watson. 124 Royal Avenue, Belfast BT1 1EB. Tel: 028 9026 4300; fax: 028 9055 4507; e-mail: bettyarnold@belfasttlelegraph.co.uk; website: www.sundaylife.co.uk

The Sunday Times

Specialist features by authoritative writers on politics, literature, art, drama, music, finance and science, as well as topical stories. Payment: Top rate for exclusive features. While *The Sunday Times* is primarily an English newspaper with its head office in London (Editor: John Witherow. 1 Virginia Street, London E1 9BD. Tel: 020 7782 4000; fax: 020 7583 9504; website: www.timesonline.co.uk), it has an increasingly important presence in Ireland. Irish address: Bishop's Square, Redmond's Hill, Dublin 2. Tel: 01 479 2424.

Sunday Tribune

Features to follow house style. Editor: Noirin Hegarty, nhegarty@tribune.ie. Tribune Publications plc, 15 Lr Baggot Street, Dublin 2. Tel: 01 661 5555; fax: 01 661 5302; e-mail: editorial@tribune.ie; website: www.tribune.ie

With a weekly circulation in excess of 140,000 The Alpha Newspaper Group is the largest newspaper group in the Irish Midlands and Northern Ireland. Its head office is situated in The Linen Green, Moygashel, Dungannon BT 71 1HB. Tel: Dungannon 048 8772 2274; fax: Dungannon 048 8775 2439; tel: London 0044 2079 3172 11; e-mail: midtrib@iol.ie; website: www.ulsternet-ni.co.uk.

Antrim Guardian 048 9446 2624
Armagh Advertiser 048 3752 2639
Ballycastle Chronicle 048 2076 1282
Ballyclare Gazette 048 9335 2967
Ballymoney Chronicle 048 2766 2354
Carrickfergus Advertiser 048 9336 3651
Cerdac Print 048 8772 2274
Coleraine Chronicle 048 7034 3344
Coleraine Constitution 048 7034 3344
County Down Outlook 048 4063 0781
Donegal Reporter 048 7188 6869
Larne Gazette 048 2827 7450
Longford News 043 46342
Limavady Chronicle 048 7776 2130
Midland Tribune Birr 0509 20003
Midland Tribune Roscrea 0505 23747
Northern Constitution Limavady 048 7776 2130
Northern Constitution Magherafelt 048 7963 2686
Roscommon Champion 090 6625051
Strabane Weekly News 048 7188 6869
The Outlook Kilkeel 048 4176 9995

The North Coast Leader 048 7034 3344
Tullamore Tribune 0506 21152
Tyrone Courier Cookstown 048 8676 6692
Tyrone Courier Dungannon 048 8772 2271
Tyrone Constitution Omagh 048 8224 2721
Tyrone Printing Moygashel 048 8772 2274
Ulster Gazette Armagh City 048 3752 2639

Look out for local papers which are in the market for local news stories and news features.

Herald AM, Free commuter paper. Daily. Relevant features. Payment by arrangement. Editor: Ronan Price. Independent House, 27-32 Talbot Street, Dublin 1. Tel: 01 705 5333; fax 01 872 0304; e-mail: hnews@unison.independent.ie; website: www.unison.ie.

LifeTimes, published fortnightly, 26a Phibsboro Place, Phibsboro, Dublin 7. Tel: 01 830 6667; fax: 01 830 6833; e-mail: lifetimes@dna.ie.

Metro, Dublin daily. Free on DART. Opportunities for freelancers who follow existing house style. E-mail idea plus first two paragraphs to news@metroireland.ie. Payment by negotiation. Embassy House, Herbert Park Lane, Dublin 4. Tel: 01 637 5900.

The Southside People, *The Northside People*, as well as *Northside People East* and *Northside People West* – all part of The Dublin People Newspaper Group catering for the suburbs of Dublin. 80/83 Omni Park, S.C. Santry, Dublin 9. Tel: 01 862 1611; fax: 01 862 1626; websites: www.southsidepeople.ie and www.northsidepeople.ie, respectively.

MAGAZINES

Listed below in alphabetical order are some of the magazines which are receptive to freelance contributions. Before approaching any of the commissioning features editors, it's advisable to study several copies of your chosen magazine so that you'll have an informed knowledge of its contents. Remember that advertising is as revealing as editorial content.

Books Ireland, 11 Newgrove Avenue, Dublin 4. Tel: 01 269 2185; e-mail: booksi@eircom.net. Editor: Jeremy Addis; features editor: Shirley Kelly. Reviews of Irish interest, Irish published and Irish author books; as well as articles of interest to librarians, booksellers and readers. Length: 800-1,400 words. Founded 1976. BI is also of use to aspiring writers not so much as a market for articles but as a market research source – who's publishing what and at what level, etc.

The Dubliner, 23 Wicklow Street, Dublin 2. Tel: 01 635 9822; e-mail: editor@thedubliner.ie; website: www.thedubliner.ie. Editor: Trevor White. Trendy city magazine interested in pieces on dining out, Irish culture, what's on, etc. Preliminary approach with idea by e-mail. Payment by negotiation. Founded 2001.

The Dublin Review, PO Box 7948, Dublin 1. Tel/fax: 01 678 8627; e-mail: brendan_barrington@yahoo.com; website: www.thedublinreview.com. Editor: Brendan Barrington. Essays, criticism, reportage and fiction. Payment by arrangement. Founded 2000.

Film Ireland, Filmbase, Curved Street, Temple Bar, Dublin 2. Tel: 01 671 1303; fax: 01 679 6717; e-mail: editor@filmbase.ie; website: www.filmireland.net. Editor: Lir Mac Cárthaigh. Bi-monthly €5. Special reports, interviews. Founded 1987.

Fortnight, An independent Review of Politics and the Arts. 11 University Road, Belfast, BT 7 1NA. Tel: 028 9023 2353/9032 4141; e-mail: editor@fortnight.org; website: www.fortnight.org. Editor: Rudie Goldsmith. Monthly £2.50. Current affairs analysis, reportage, opinion pieces, cultural criticism, book reviews, poems. Payment by arrangement. Founded 1970.

The Furrow, St Patrick's College, Maynooth, Co. Kildare. Tel: 01 708 3741; fax 01 708 3908; e-mail: furrow.office@may.ie; website: www.thefurrow.ie. Editor: Rev Ronan Drury. Monthly €2.30. Religious, pastoral, theological, social articles. Length: Up to 3,000 words. Payment average €20 per 450 words. Founded 1950.

Hot Press, 13 Trinity Street, Dublin 2. Tel: 01 241 1500; fax: 01 241 1539; e-mail: info@hotpress.ie; website: www.hotpress.com; Editor: Niall Stokes. Fortnightly €3.50. High-quality investigative stories, punchily written offbeat pieces, focusing on politics, sex, religion, music, sport. Length: Varies. Payment by negotiation. Founded 1977.

Hotel and Catering Review, Jemma Publications Ltd, Marino House, 52 Glasthule Road, Sandycove, Co. Dublin. Tel: 01 280 0000; fax: 01 280 1818; e-mail: s.grennan@jemma.ie. Editor: Sarah Grennan. Monthly, €79.45 pa. Length: Varies. Payment by negotiation.

Image, Crofton Hall, 22 Crofton Road, Dun Laoghaire, Co. Dublin. Tel: 01 280 8415; fax: 01 280 8309; website: www.image.ie; Editor: Melanie Morris. Monthly. Up-market features on fashion, beauty, women, living and the home. Preliminary approach advised. Length: Varies. Payment by negotiation.

Ireland's Own, Channing House, Upper Rowe Street, Wexford. Tel: 053 40140; fax: 053 40192; e-mail: irelands.own@peoplenews.ie. Monthly specials editor: Phil

Murphy; weekly issues editor: Sean Nolan. Editorial requirements: Non-fiction features with strong Irish background, historical and general interest in region of 750-1,000 words, ideally accompanied by reproducible illustration; also filler items of 400 words or less. Weekly €1. Payment €50/€60 per feature; €15/€20 per filler. Founded 1902.

Ireland of the Welcomes, Fáilte Ireland, Baggot Street Bridge, Dublin 2. Tel: 01 602 4000; fax: 01 602 4335; e-mail: iow@failteireland.ie; website: www.irelandofthewelcomes.com. Bi-monthly €3.50. Editor: Letitia Pollard. Designed to attract visitors to Ireland. Features on history, crafts, music, sports and people. Preliminary approach advised. Length 1,200-1,800 words. Payment by arrangement. Founded 1952.

The Irish Book Review, Ashbrook House, 10 Main Street, Raheny, Dublin 5. Tel: 01 851 1459; e-mail: info@irishbookreview.com; website: irishbookreview.com. Editor: Eugene O'Brien. Quarterly. As title suggests, reviews Irish books as well as author profiles. Preliminary approach advised.

Irish Farmers Journal, Irish Farm Centre, Bluebell, Dublin 12. Tel: 01 419 9500; fax: 01 452 0876; e-mail: editdeot@ifj.ie; website: www.farmersjournal.ie. Editor: Matthew Dempsey. Weekly €2. Readable articles on farming. Length: 700-1,000 words. Payment by negotiation. Founded 1948.

Irish Medical Times, 24-26 Upper Ormond Quay, Dublin 7. Tel: 01 817 6300; fax: 01 817 6345; e-mail: colin.kerr@imt.ie; website: www.imt.ie. Editor: Colin Kerr. Weekly €5.75. Free to full-time practising doctors. Medical features, also humorous articles with a medical slant. Length: Approx 1,000 words.

Irish Pages: A Journal of Contemporary Writing, The Linen Hall Library, 17 Donegal Square, Belfast BT150B. Tel: 028 9064 1644; e-mail: irishpages@yahoo.co.uk; website: www.irishpages.org. Editor: Chris Agee. Bi-annual €14/£10.

Short fiction, poetry, creative non-fiction, essays, memoir, essay reviews, nature writing, translations, literary journalism and biographical, historical and scientific writing with a literary slant. Publishes writing from Ireland and abroad. Payment by arrangement. Founded 2002.

Irish Printer, Jemma Publications Ltd, 52 Glasthule Road, Sandycove, Co. Dublin. Tel: 01 280 0000; fax: 01 280 1818; e-mail: f.venturini@jemma.ie. Editor: Fabio Venturini. Monthly. Features of interest to the printing industry. Length: 800-1,000 words. Payment by negotiation.

Irish Tatler, 2 Clanwilliam Court, Lower Mount Street, Dublin 2. Tel: 01 662 3158; fax: 01 661 9757; e-mail: jstevens@harmonia.ie. Editor: Jennifer Stevens. Features on beauty, interiors, fashion, cookery, current affairs, celebrity interviews. Length: 2,000-4,000 words. Payment by negotiation.

Living It, Black Dot Publishing, CPG House, Glenageary Office Park, Dun Laoghaire, Co. Dublin. Tel: 01 202 4522; fax: 01 284 7584; e-mail: anna@blackdotpublishing.com; website: www.blackdotpublishing.com. Editor: Anna Clarke. Lifestyle magazine aimed at the over-50s. Initial approach with feature ideas by e-mail. Payment by negotiation.

Magill, 1-4 Swift Alley, Dublin 8. Tel: 01 416 7834; e-mail: magill@bandf.net. Editor: Eamon Delaney. Monthly. Cutting-edge current affairs, politics, business.

Poetry Ireland Review/Éigse Éireann, 2 Proud's Lane, off St Stephens Green, Dublin 2. Tel: 01 478 9974; fax: 01 478 0205; e-mail: poetry@iol.ie. website: www.poetryireland.ie. Editor: Peter Sirr. Poetry and related features by arrangement. Quarterly. €7.99. Founded 1981.

Reality, Orwell Road, Rathgar, Dublin 6. Tel: 01 492 2488; fax: 01 492 2654; e-mail: info@redemptoristpublications.com: website: www.redemptoristpublications.com. Editor: Rev Gerry Moloney. Monthly €1.30. Articles on modern life –

family, youth, religion and leisure. Length: Approximately 1,000 words. Payment by arrangement. Founded 1936.

Social and Personal, 21st Century Media Ltd, 19 Nassau Street, Dublin 2. Tel: 01 633 3993; fax: 01 633 4353; e-mail: editor@socialandpersonal.ie; website: www.socialandpersonal.ie. Editor: PJ Gibbons. Monthly up-market social and lifestyle magazine. Initial approach with feature ideas to editor by e-mail. Payment by negotiation.

Studies, An Irish Quarterly Review, 35 Lower Leeson Street, Dublin 2. Tel: 01 676 6785; fax: 01 676 2984; e-mail: studies@jesuit.ie; website: ww.studiesirishreview.com. Editor: Rev Fergus O'Donoghue. Quarterly €7.50. Articles written by specialists for the general reader on social comment, literature, history, the arts, as well as critical book reviews. Length: 4,000 words. Preliminary letter. Founded 1912.

Technology Ireland, Enterprise Ireland, Strand Road, Dublin 4. Tel: 01 206 6337; fax: 01 206 6342; e-mail: technology.ireland.ie; website: www.technologyireland.ie. Editors: Tom Kennedy, Sean Duke. Monthly, €48 pa. Articles, reviews, news on current business, innovation and technology. Length: 1,500-2,000 words. Payment by negotiation. Founded 1969.

U Magazine, Harmonia, 2 Clanwilliam Court, Lower Mount Street, Dublin 2. Tel: 01 662 3158; fax: 01 661 9757; e-mail: dokeeffe@harmonia.ie. Editor: Deirdre O'Keeffe. Monthly, €41.16 pa. Aimed at 18-to-25-year-old market. Features on celebrity interviews, talent profiles, real-life stories, sex and relationship features, plus regulars of the club scene, movies, music and film, as well as travel and interiors, health, food, horoscopes. Material mostly commissioned but suitable ideas by e-mail welcomed. Payment by negotiation. Founded 1978.

Ulster Business, Greer Publications, 5B Edgewater Business Park, Edgewater Road, Belfast Harbour Estate, Belfast

BT3 9 JQ. Tel: 028 9078 3223; fax: 028 9078 3210; e-mail: russellcampbell@greenpublicaions.com; website: www.ulsterbusiness.com. Editor: Russell Campbell. Monthly £2.30. Feature–based with general business-related editorial for management level and above. Specially commissions most material but will consider unsolicited material. Welcomes ideas for articles and features. Length: 800-1,500 words. Payment by negotiation. Founded 1987.

Ulster Grocer, Greer Publications, 5B Edgewater Business Park, Edgewater Road, Belfast Harbour Estate, Belfast BT3 9 JQ. Tel: 028 9078 3200; fax: 028 9078 3210; e-mail: kathyj@writenow.prestel.co.uk. Editor: Kathy Jensen. Monthly controlled circulation. Topical features (1,000-1,500 words) on food/grocery retailing, company spotlights, personal interviews, category features and consumer/market insights; news (200 words) with a Northern Ireland basis. All features commissioned. Payment: Features: £275; product news: £160. Founded 1972.

Village, 44 Westland Row, Dublin 2. Tel 01 642 5050; e-mail: editor@villagemagazine.ie; website: www.villagemagazine.ie. Editor: Vincent Browne. Cutting-edge current affairs weekly. Approach editor by e-mail with ideas. Payment by negotiation.

Woman's Way, Harmonia, Clanwilliam House, Clanwilliam Place, Lower Mount Street, Dublin 2. Tel: 01 662 3158. Editor: Marie Kelly welcomes approaches for suitable features by e-mail giving a brief outline of your idea. Suitability can be gleaned by reading back issues of the magazine. Send to mkelly@harmonia.ie. Payment by negotiation. Weekly €1.30.

3

the magic of radio

'Radio gives birth to a million images in a million brains.'
Peggy Noone, US presidential speech writer

While radio is regarded in some quarters as the Cinderella of media, it has a huge – and often unlikely – fan base of all ages. Its main popularity seems to stem from the fact that it offers more variety than television and is more intimate than the printed word. Making radio programmes is considerably cheaper than making programmes for television, which means radio stations can afford to be more experimental.

For instance, a radio play set in the various locations of Rome, London and Paris is as inexpensive to produce as a play set solely against a kitchen backdrop. Why? Because the essence of Rome can be conjured up by church bells, London by Big Ben and Paris by the music of the cancan dance. And the various decades can be spanned with little more than clever production.

One of the joys of radio is that it forces us to invest in dramatising whatever action is happening in our heads. And in these days of constant texting, e-mailing and quick mobile calls, none of which engage the imagination, the creative accomplishment of dramatising and visualising actions is positively euphoric.

'People have stories to tell and RTÉ is one of the main outlets by which people *can*, *may* and *do* tell their own and others' stories,' says Seamus Hosey, producer of Radio Arts, Features and Drama Programmes with RTÉ Radio. 'Since 1926 we have broadcast thousands of hours of quality material in prose, poetry, drama, discussion, documentary, reportage and fiction that draws on the experiences, real or imagined, of Irish people, at home and abroad.'

TALKS

'A lively freelance market exists in RTÉ Radio,' says Hosey. 'Freelance work is accepted by such programmes as 'Sunday Miscellany', 'The Quiet Corner', 'The Enchanted Way' (poetry only), 'The Living Word' and, from time to time, by competitions featured on the Ryan Tubridy, Gerry Ryan and Pat Kenny Shows. 'Rattlebag' occasionally runs The Poetry Slam Open Mike event and other programmes draw on the creative talents of freelance and professional writers. Payment varies and more details can usually be found on the appropriate programme website.'

For those interested in writing for radio, it's easier to make your debut with a short piece rather than a story, play or documentary. But don't think short means easy, though the easiest way of getting to know the requirements of the producers and what works in the broadcast medium is to listen to several of the programmes with an objective ear and an analytical mind, paying special attention to subject matter, construction, choice of words, frequency of word pictures, etc. and then apply what you've heard to yourself and your own writing.

Both RTÉ Radio 1's 'A Living Word' (ninety seconds of speech, approx 200 words) and 'Sunday Miscellany' (approximately 650-750 words) and Lyric FM's 'Quiet Quarter' (three to five minutes long, 450-550 words) serve as an illustration of what's best in writing for the radio.

Scripts for these programmes have been described as 'cameos of perfection', and to reach that stage they require careful thought, writing, rewriting, editing and revision, taking into consideration how your script sounds when spoken as well as content. When it's as perfect as you can make it, record it, listen back and adjust, if necessary.

The pieces are read in studio by the author, who should allow adequate rehearsal time to achieve a professional standard of delivery, checking intonation, pacing, pauses and unusual pronunciations. As beginners to the recording studio, the main adjustment is to slow down pace of delivery, to pause after full stops and commas, to raise your voice at the beginning of each sentence and lower it towards the end.

'A Living Word' goes out from Monday to Friday at 6.40 a.m. on RTÉ Radio 1; Lyric FM's 'Quiet Quarter' is also broadcast from Monday to Friday at 10.40 a.m. Both these programmes use the same contributor for the five days.

'Sunday Miscellany', which is broadcast on Sunday mornings at 9.10 a.m., is one of the longest-running programmes on RTÉ Radio 1 and has a dedicated following.

The guidelines for writers wishing to contribute to these programmes can be found on www.rte.ie and www.lyricfm@rte.ie They include:

• Conversational in tone and written for the spoken word in first person wherever possible.
• Provide imagery of word pictures in simple but not simplistic language.
• Avoid vague abstractions, over-literary language, copious facts and figures and over-usage of adjectives and adverbs.
• Keep sentences short and meaning clear and ensure there is a clear narrative running through your piece.
• Remember: radio is an intimate medium where you're talking to one person.

RADIO IS...

In a poll conducted by *The Daily Telegraph*, Paul McCartney summed up his feelings for radio: 'Setting the imagination free! Stimulating parts not normally reached by other media. Good for grey matter.' Mick Jagger said he loved 'radio's very simple technology, available worldwide, no national boundaries, distinctions. Leaves you free to do other things.' Many of the others polled mentioned freedom, flexibility, limitless possibilities for the imagination and the chance to take radio with you. More were taken by the imperceptible way radio can become a friend.

Terry Wogan believes that 'as a presenter you can get into people's thoughts and achieve a one-to-one almost personal contact that's impossible on television.' According to the late, great DJ John Peel, 'It's better not to try to analyse what is a most complex relationship. There's something mystical about sharing an intimate experience with people you'll never know. This applies equally whether you're a broadcaster or a listener, I think.' Many radio buffs would agree with these sentiments.

Radio is hugely about word pictures. It forces us to invest more, to dramatise action in our heads, never more so than in the short story or radio play, which have the extraordinary power to create a whole world in a matter of minutes. Why and how can this be so? For the simple reason that we engage considerably more with material we bring our imagination to.

For those of you interested in writing for radio, the most important fact to keep in mind is that writing to be listened to has to be written differently from material that will be read. With radio it's how a script sounds, not how it looks on the page. The best radio writing frequently looks awful in print, with incomplete sentences, conversational words and repetitive phrases. Good radio is simple, yet sophisticated – an intimate medium of personal word pictures.

THE RADIO SHORT STORY

What kind of short story works best for radio? According to Di Speirs, Executive Producer Readings at BBC Radio 4, 'It's hard to be definitive. Every rule can be broken if the writing or the characters are strong enough. However, a successful short story whether read or heard needs to be more a snapshot of a moment and to convey more than it covers. A world seen through a quick glancing light works extraordinarily well.' She also makes the point that as most of the stories go out in the middle of the afternoon, when children may be listening, the BBC will not broadcast anything offensive or unsuitable in content or language for a daytime audience.

RTÉ's main story outlets are the series broadcast, usually in early spring, drawn from the winners and runners-up of the annual Francis MacManus competition, and the popular Fiction Fifteen, which goes out Sunday around teatime. While initially this was targeted towards teenage listeners, it has become compulsive listening for radio aficionados of any age.

'New writers are encouraged to enter competitions such as The Francis MacManus Short Story Competition,' says Hosey. 'Established twenty years ago, it has received more than 16,000 original short stories and broadcast over 500 stories by new and emerging writers, many of whom have gone on to become established writers – novelists, short story writers, playwrights, poets and acclaimed creative forces at home and abroad.'

When writing a short story for radio, bear the following in mind:

• The audience can't look back to the beginning, so the plot must be clear and the characters not too numerous.
• Jumps in time can be hard to negotiate for even the most skilled listener.

- Unbroken lyrical prose can wash over the audience, who will probably be busy doing other things at the same time.
- Dialogue is often the ideal way to break up long passages and to rekindle the audience's attention.

RADIO PLAYS

BBC Radio 4 commissions programmes twice a year and at each commissioning round, it publishes a set of guidelines. Log on to www.bbc.co.uk/drama for updated guidelines and also for tips on writing radio drama, some of which are listed below.

If you're interested in pitching a proposal, ensure your pitch meets the criteria of the checklist below. (Note: It would be highly unusual for a newcomer to radio drama to be commissioned on an initial pitch.)
• Subject of play.
• Synopsis.
• How the story will be told.
• Ending.

In addition, for dramatisations or adaptations of stage plays, clarify:
• How the story will be told for radio.
• Why it's suited to radio.

For serials or series, it's important to detail the following:
• The construction of the work.
• A detailed synopsis should outline the development of character and plot over the episodes, as well as various plot-lines.
• Tone of the work.
• Situation comedy requires full details of the characters and dynamics of relationships that are essential to its success and these must prove strong enough to endure repetition over several episodes and perhaps several series.

And about you, the writer:
• Are you experienced in writing for radio? If so, include previous credits.
• If you're new to writing for radio, even though you may be experienced in other aspects of writing, you should include

either a full script written on spec or sample scenes demon-strating that you can write for the medium.

Anyone interested in submitting an idea for comedy or drama to Radio 4 should contact either The Writersroom, BBC's online resource for writing drama, an independent producer or a BBC department. Would-be dramatists are asked *not* to send material direct to the network.

While there are not the same opportunities in Irish broad-casting as in the UK and Northern Ireland for radio drama, RTÉ does have regular slots. Keep an eye on the website, as requirements for drama change regularly. There's also the annual P.J. O'Connor Award, which broadcasts a selection of winning plays and has been the starting point for many aspiring playwrights.

Guidelines for writing drama for RTÉ Radio 1 can be downloaded from the website at www.rte.ie/radio1/drama.

Under *Some Practical Points on Construction*, the would-be playwright is advised that there is no formula for writing a successful radio play. 'It requires the techniques of good dra-matic writing, plus an imaginative awareness of the restric-tions and advantages of a medium where nothing is seen. It is only by listening to radio plays that a writer can judge what works and what doesn't.'

You can also download a sample script from the same website. It is the required layout for submitting to RTÉ and represents one minute playing time, including music and effects. A page of script laid out in this format usually runs to one minute.

Further on is a sample page from my script for *Time & Straw*. I'm using my own radio play, based on the life of Irish designer Eileen Gray, as an example.

Before I began the actual writing of the script, I had my research completed, knew the story forwards and backwards and had written a synopsis, followed by scene sequence and short character sketches.

The story broke into seventeen scenes of varying length set in New York, London, Paris and County Wexford from the period of 1912 to 1972. It was to be an hour-long play with a running time of 57 minutes in which, through dialogue, the characters would have to tell the story and forward the action.

The characters I chose from the vast cast that peopled both Gray's life and my fictional take on the Gray story included Eileen Gray; Robert Walker, expert in antiques, journalist and Doucet's son; his mother, Nancy; Colette, the French writer and Gray's best friend; Jacques Doucet, who had long loved Gray and was her mentor; Louise Dany, Eileen's maid; and James MacLaren Smith, Eileen's father.

As a matter of note, I used as few stage directions as possible.

Scene 1 takes place in 1972, in Robert Walker's apartment in New York, with Robert and Nancy Walker. Nancy learns that Doucet, who she has always loved, is dead. His collection has been auctioned. The Le Destin screen has broken all records for 'modern antiques'.

Scene 6 is set in 1913 at a pavement café in Paris with Colette, Doucet and Gray. Gray, who has returned from a flight, plans to design the lacquer screen which becomes Le Destin.

Scene 8, on the family estate in County Wexford in 1888, shows the relationship between Eileen and her father as well as family history.

Sample Page:
Scene 2 – Paris – Interior – Eileen Gray's apartment. November 1972. Noon

FX: Phone ringing. Footsteps along tiled floor

1. *Louise Dany* Allo. Ou est ici? **(phone talking)** Oh, oui (speaking throughout in French-accented English) I remember **(phone talking)** Non it is not possible. **(phone talking)** Not even with an introduction. Mademoiselle Gray does not receive visitors **(phone talking)** We 'ave no comment on the sale.

2. *Eileen Gray* **(querulously from the salon)** Dorothy, who is it?

3. *Louise Dany* One moment, sir. **(pause, raised voice pitching back to salon)** Mr Robert Walker. Again. You remember the American collector?

4. *Eileen Gray* Of course. I haven't lost my memory. What does he want?

5. *Louise Dany* The same as yesterday. To visit you.

6. *Eileen Gray* I'll see him. Today. If nothing else, his persistence deserves reward. Tell him to come after my siesta.

7. *Louise Dany* Monsieur Walker. Mademoiselle Gray will see you this afternoon at five o'clock. You wish the address **(phone talking)** Bon. You know where. **(replaces phone, returns to salon)** What made you change your mind, mademoiselle?

4

the
short
story

'In my beginning is my end.' T.S. Eliot

Short stories are a wonderful, innovative, creative exercise in writing discipline. They afford the writer an unlimited licence of creativity. There are no set patterns – the plotless short story, the prose poem, the magazine love story or crime story can work just as well as the plotted or unplotted novella.

The short story frequently involves one clearly defined incident. It can be defined as a snapshot in time, i.e. the reader knows the characters have an ongoing life both before the story begins and after it finishes.

A classic example of the modern short story is Anne Enright's 'Shaft', the story of a pregnant woman who rides up in a lift to the seventh floor with a man who for the most part is silently curious about her condition. Enright chose a lift as the setting because of its womb-like containment – a ploy which she considers works well with the short story – and the shaft of both the title and the lift is representative of the umbilical cord. Enright says:

> People often ask where I get my ideas from, sometimes they say 'inspiration'. 'Where do you get your inspiration from?'. I have a very ordinary view of where stories come from – they do not descend from heaven, they are made. Sometimes they are made out of an argument you are having in your head with the world, or with someone in the world, an impulse you have to say 'No it is not like that', or 'It is more complicated than that'. Sometimes you want to catch something about a person, or a character – any person – and you want to put it down on the page and see where it leads you, and what that might mean.
>
> Most often I work from a first sentence. This sentence does not walk, fully formed into my head. I am sitting, writing about anything, thinking 'this isn't much' and, about two paragraphs down, I get my first sentence. Then I look at it for a while. 'Ah,' I say. Then I start again.

The first sentence is the voice of the story; this is the person, the attitude, and often the question that will get you through the next few thousand words. I read and reread the first few paragraphs to find out what the person's problem is here. Short stories can be solutions – often unexpected ones.

Some stories are character led, others deal with a situation, or an idea (adultery, for example), many deal with a particular emotion I experienced once and want to recreate.

The voice in the short story is never me. People can find this confusing.

The characters do not exist either. Some are completely fictional – these in general relate to an archetype of some kind (which is not the same thing as a cliché), some are constructed out of people I know, like golems, or Frankenstein's monster, I put someone's smile under someone else's bald head, and if I get it right, the whole thing stands up and starts to move. Other characters just walk in, unannounced, like the first line – but this happens only after an amount of work.

I think I am saying that you do not start with inspiration but, when you work, you leave yourself open to it, should it arrive.

Short story writing is a demanding, precise and disciplined genre, but its construction and compilation from the germ of an idea to polished perfection is one of the most exciting and rewarding writing experiences and an exercise favoured by a variety of writers of all types of fiction.

Yet short stories, beloved by the book-buying public for their ability to be dipped into, are spurned by the majority of Irish and UK publishers for their lack of commerciality, and over the past decade, the number of magazines publishing short stories is in decline. It's a different situation in the US, where the short story is king. And indeed, courtesy of BBC Radio 4 and BBC World Service, as well as RTÉ Radio 1, the radio short story has never fallen into decline. Anne Enright says:

> I am unusual in that my first published book was a collection of short stories. It is much easier to sell a novel. Even now, when my work goes into the *New Yorker* and *Granta* – which are the two best places for short pieces on either side of the Atlantic – my publishers tell me that collections of short stories are 'worth nothing' and they 'cost more to produce than they bring in'. These are the facts: you can get whiny about it, or you can make a living. I fund my stories with my novels and I fund my novels with non-fiction, journalism and teaching. I like all of these things. Some ideas are the shape of an essay, some are the shape of a novel. A few (not all that many, actually) are the exact shape of a short story.

For the beginner, the short story is a more manageable length than a novel and can be written (though not necessarily edited to a professional standard) in a relevantly short space of time. Enright says:

> I have stories on my computer screen for years. No story gets finished in under six months. They need silence. To balance that, I have lots of beginnings and fragments to work on at any given time. Also, when it does come to the crunch, I can do the final draft in a week.

I'm frequently asked how long is a short story. That varies from writer to writer and from publication to publication. Commercial short stories usually run from 2,500 to 3,000 words, mine usually coming in under or around 3,000 words. A chewy short story is 5,000 words long. A long short story is 10,000 words long. Fifteen thousand is a piece that doesn't really know what it is – it is very hard to end something that long. Thirty thousand is a novella, which is another thing again.

A short story frequently starts with a kernel of fact – the idea of the pregnant woman in the lift appealed to Enright – which becomes cloaked in inspiration and imagination and is then fused to technique and finally style. Technique is mainly acquired by practice; our instinctive writing style is inherent within us but can always be improved on.

Enright says she prefers not to be too 'zennish' about analysing the whys, wherefores and hows of her construction of short stories, which have appeared in *The Paris Review* as well as *The New Yorker* and *Granta*, in most of the notable anthologies of Irish fiction in addition to being broadcast on BBC's Radio 4. Her first collection, *The Portable Virgin*, won the Rooney Prize for Irish Literature.

Short stories are usually read in one sitting and the most successful draw their readers along by the magnetic power of the anticipated conclusion. They are end-orientated, i.e. we begin with the expectation of soon reaching the conclusion. Enright comments:

> Short stories end; they believe in and tend towards some kind of ending. It is essential that this ending should not be closed. The important thing is not the last line, but the silence after the last line – it is the quality of that silence that makes the story work.
>
> Old-fashioned stories have a formal ending – a 'sting in the tail', or some kind of 'point'. Modern short stories sometimes end with the fact that nothing has changed, after all: it is still raining, the world goes on. This ending bores me to tears.
>
> My own early stories tend towards some sort of metaphor, and stop once it is achieved. My recent stories end with something – often something unexpected – becoming clear.

Much of Enright's work is about the gap between how things feel inside and how they look outside. She says she's not sure where she got this despairing insideness of a person while staying outside. 'I suppose Beckett does. I only write what I can.'

Ciaran Carty, a *Sunday Tribune* journalist specialising in the arts, has been editing *New Irish Writing* and selecting stories for inclusion in the Hennessey Award for the past eighteen years. He receives an average of 100 submissions each month and chooses one for publication on the first Sunday of each month.

And how does he make his choice? Carty says:

> A story chooses itself. It has a voice that draws you in and makes you read on. This matters more than a plot or a theme (not that these are not important). Of course it's an intuitive thing, and sometimes a voice is so strange and different that it may be hard to detect, but once it makes itself heard, the experience is perhaps all the more rewarding.
>
> Over the years, there hasn't been that much change in style. Perhaps the writing is more confident and aware. The content, of course, keeps changing in terms of issues and what's happening in the world, but the better stories are rarely a response to current headlines but rather reflect a particular sensibility. While the voices vary with each writer, the overall quality is probably much the same. We had just as much difficulty trying to decide what to leave out of the second Hennessy anthology, published in 2005, as we had with the first, ten years ago.

Does he have any golden tips for writers? 'The only tip is to keep writing, don't be afraid to have someone else read your story and don't fuss about it too long – get it out there. A story doesn't exist until it has a reader.'

POINTS TO PONDER

- Make sure you enjoy the process of writing – your enjoyment spills into your work.
- Start small and go for detail.
- Learn to look and use objects around you for inspiration.
- Try to use suggestiveness and gestures to give a sense of character and story.
- Do your research. Avoid making factual errors when you describe an object or place.
- Beginnings and endings should have a powerful impact – plan to revisit them.
- Be prepared to work on your dialogue by listening to conversations.
- Look at a critical point in someone's life or focus on heightened moments.
- Ensure the story is carefully observed and quickly told.
- Leave your reader thinking – perhaps with a surprise twist.

FIRST DRAFT

The best modern short stories convey information by suggestion rather than by fact, and in Enright's case, fetish. 'I like to fetishise objects,' she said in an interview with *The Independent* in March 2000. 'I find if you stare at them long enough they become funny. You stop being able to "read" them.' Her characters have a terrible time with objects and choosing. One shoplifts, while another is utterly lost in the physical world.

One of Enright's achingly funny and yet tragic stories concerns a woman selling handbags who gets obsessed with matching bags with customers. According to *The Independent* interview, 'Her work presents physical objects with upset hilarity. A roll of ham on a plate looms ever more disturbingly at her characters who despair of dealing with it, or after a while even of seeing it adequately.'

Writers teeming with ideas and plots, characters leaping for inclusion and locations all jostling for ascendancy should thank their lucky stars and set everything down as quickly as possible while the inspiration is flowing. Hard as it may be to believe when the creative juices are in full flow, this brand of inspiration is short-lived and should be treated as a rare and beautiful gift.

While you're in full writing flight, don't worry about structure, spelling or punctuation. Maeve Binchy maintains that at this stage, flow should only be interrupted by something as serious as the house on fire! If you do stop, even briefly, to make that much-needed coffee, the momentum can be difficult to recapture.

For those less blessed with all-consuming inspiration, while it's a good idea to write a synopsis and have an idea of the ending before starting to write, it's equally important to be flexible. One of the most wonderful aspects of writing fiction is that there are no hard and fast rules. Oftentimes the apparently unworkable works.

As characters emerge and come to life, they frequently determine different conflicts. A short story is not a description or a character sketch, or indeed a beautifully written set piece about a location – pitfalls that often beset the beginner. While both description and characterisation play an integral part, the most memorable short stories have conflict with crises increasing in intensity as the story progresses, such as in Enright's 'Shaft', where the tension between the woman and the man in the lift was at times almost unbearable.

EDITING, REWRITING, REVISING

When you've finished that first draft, take a breather. Ideally put your story away for a few days. In a recent newspaper interview, William Trevor maintained that he often rested a piece of writing for a year. It's a rare story or indeed any other form of writing that doesn't need editing.

Many writers enjoy the editing process even more than the drafting, though not Anne Enright, who says, 'I do not write, I only rewrite. I edit all the time. (The trick is not to edit before, or nothing gets written at all.)'

Editing at whatever stage calls for honest spadework, ruthless pruning, streamlining for style and seeking readability, or in the case of the radio short story, listenability. Whether your story is to be read or listened to, a helpful way to achieve these twin prerequisites is by reading your manuscript aloud. Even better, if you have a recorder, tape it and play it back. Awkward construction, words that don't work and blurriness are immediately obvious.

A word to the uninitiated writers: while our families and friends will invariably be overjoyed at our writing, laud our brilliance and be full of support for our endeavours, unless they're professionals themselves, take care about sharing your work with them at editing stage. Because they haven't the skill, they can't listen or read with professional ears or eyes.

CHECKLIST

- Is the title arresting, interesting and appropriate?
- Does the opening make immediate and intimate contact with the reader/listener, demanding continuation?
- Does the story begin in the right place? Many first drafts begin too soon. The best of today's short stories dive into the narrative without explanation, preamble or elaborate introduction. Chekhov famously said that most short stories benefited by jettisoning the first half. Avoid beginning your story by filling in the past.
- Have you chosen the right viewpoint character? Viewpoint characters should have a stake in the outcome.
- Can the reader/listener identify with the viewpoint character?
- Is your plot tight? Plot begins when a problem occurs that requires reaction from a character. As necessary, create and heighten suspense and sustain conflict.
- Does your plot have structure? Structure requires a beginning, middle and end.
- Does plot have pace? Varying the pace brings energy to your story.
- Is the ending satisfying? Usually a satisfying ending depends on the main character/protagonist solving his or her own problem.
- Lastly, remember to show rather than tell where possible.

Anne Enright's tips for short story writers is to read everything by the following authors: Anton Chekhov, Frank O'Connor, Raymond Carver, Alice Munro and Flannery O'Connor. You might also read Katherine Mansfield, Grace Paley, *The Bloody Chamber* by Angela Carter and *Dubliners* by James Joyce.

For information on where to have short stories published, see the Outlets for Short Stories below and Chapter 3, The Magic of Radio, for information on writing short stories for radio.

OUTLETS FOR SHORT STORIES

Without a doubt, the most prestigious magazine outlets for short stories in the world are *The New Yorker* and *Granta*.

The New Yorker, 4 Times Square, New York, NY 10036. Submissions to *The New Yorker* should be sent either by regular mail or as part of the body of an e-mail to fiction@newyorker.com. The magazine responds to all submissions but warns that due to volume, this may take up to three months.

Granta, London: 2/3 Hanover Yard, Noel Road, London, N18BE. Tel: 0044 207 704 9776; e-mail: info@granta.com. Editor: Ian Jack, e-mail: ijack@granta.com. More details from www.granta.com.

Granta, New York: 1755 Broadway, 5th Floor, New York, NY, 10019, US. Tel: 212 246 1313.

Many newcomers to short story writing envisage their work appearing in anthology or collection form. As mentioned earlier, the bad news is that collections of short stories are no longer the darlings of publishers (Anne Enright is the exception that proves the rule where writing is concerned). Usually you have to be an established author and even then they are increasingly infrequent.

The good news is that as well as the various competitions listed in Chapter 2 for short stories, essays and plays, there are still many and varied outlets for a good short story. Check the section on Presentation in Chapter 1. A professional piece of work is more likely to be looked on kindly by an overworked editor or producer – and all editors and producers are overworked – than a carelessly presented story.

Other print outlets for short stories include the following.

Image magazine, Crofton Hall, Crofton Road, Dun Laoghaire, Co. Dublin. Tel: 01 280 8415. *Image* publishes a short story or book extract each month. The choice of subject is eclectic. Short stories should be in the region of 4,000 words; book extracts are usually submitted and negotiated with the publisher. Payment is by negotiation. Entries should be submitted to Carolyn McGrath.

Ireland's Own magazine, Channing House, Upper Rowe Street, Wexford. Tel: 053 40140; fax: 053 40192; e-mail: irelands.own@peoplenews.ie. Monthly specials editor: Phil Murphy; weekly issues editor: Sean Nolan. Requirements: Fictional stories, approximately 2,000 words, written in a 'straightforward style', typifying 'a good yarn', as well as a storyline with an Irish orientation where possible. E-mail copy, with script in body of text acceptable. Payment: €65 per 2,000 words.

Sunday Tribune, 15 Lower Baggot Street, Dublin 2. tel: 01 661 5555. On the first Sunday of each month, Review section publishes a short story in the region of 2,500 words. For further details see Chapter titled Awards and Prizes for Short Stories, Essays and Plays. Monthly stories are automatically entered for Hennessey Award, announced in November.

Woman's Way, 2 Clanwilliam Crescent, Lower Mount Street, Dublin 2. Tel: 01 662 3158. Editor Marie Kelly welcomes unsolicited short stories on topics of writer's choice; wordage should be in the region of 1,600. Payment is by negotiation.

5

the
novel

'A novel is a mirror walking along a main road.' Stendhal

The best fiction achieves proportion, which can be defined as the proper relationship between description, narration and dialogue while blending together an art and a craft.

It has been said that the great novels of today have:

* great openings
* great stories
* great writing
* great themes
* great endings
* great covers.

The writer is primarily responsible for the first five points, though good editing can enhance openings, stories, writing, themes and endings. The publishers, in liason with their marketing department, are responsible for the book's cover.

As well as a great storyline, which, of course, includes great characters in a great setting with a great sense of style and technique, it requires perseverance and dedication to write a novel to the standard of professionalism where it can be considered for publication. It's as well to remember there's a lot of competition out there, but talent does out.

The majority of modern novels are primarily either plot or character led. Writers like Paul Carson and John Grisham, a doctor and lawyer turned authors, write thrillers, a genre which traditionally has been plot driven, though Patricia Cornwell has introduced Kay Scarpetta, a formidable forensic expert whose character development only adds to Cornwell's plots, and who has achieved her own official fan list under The Good Doctors.

On the other hand, Maeve Binchy and proponents of contemporary fiction, such as Patricia Scanlan, Sheila O'Flanagan and Douglas Kennedy, all write what can be loosely described as character-driven fiction, as does three-time Booker nominee Ian McEwan with his novel *Saturday* (he won in 1998 with *Amsterdam*) and D.B.C. Pierre's unforgettable first novel, *Vernon God Little*, with its fifteen-year-old narrator, which won him the Man Booker in 2003.

THE MARKET

While an original, talented, new voice such as Alice Sebold's *The Lovely Bones* and *The Time Traveller's Wife* by Audrey Niffenegger will usually out, as would-be novelists we need to get the feel of the book market, to know what's being published and by which publishers, what's making the bestseller list both in Ireland and in the UK and what type of works are being translated for the European market and sold into America. Acquiring this knowledge is called market research.

So how do you go about doing this market research for novels? Quite simply by trawling the bookshops, asking booksellers what's selling, talking to the people who buy books, finding out what kind of books they're buying and why. Some years ago there was a rash of what was called 'aga sagas', which were replaced by career-woman-makes-a-go-of-it novels. Currently the trend appears to be for multi-generation family sagas, which may well have changed too by the time this book is in print.

Obviously it's not advisable for a writer – particularly a new writer – to sit down to write a market-driven novel unless the formula has been tried, tested and proven successful and that he or she is sure of being published – unlikely if you're a new novelist. A point to remember is that it can take up to two years from acceptance to publication. The length of time to write and polish, say, the requisite 80,000 to 100,000 words is immeasurable.

Another point to bear in mind is that publishers and a writer's fans, those important people who wait for a favoured author's next book, look for consistency, like to know what they're buying and, particularly where popular women's fiction is concerned, don't like too long a time span between books.

Not only is there a sameness about former freelance journalist John Connolly's crime stories, but his hero, Charlie Parker, has become a much-loved fictional figure. Anita

Brookner's short novels are delicious pastiches of unbelievably strong romantic women. Anita Shreve's novels may be wide-spanning in their subjects, but her writing style is as individual as her fingerprints.

'Is what you want to write different to what people want to read?' was one of the questions Edwina Currie, English MP turned novelist, asked her audience at a recent seminar titled, 'How to Make Money Writing Fiction'. It was a good question and one many writers don't give a lot of thought to, much less root for the right answer. It's vital to be aware of this. If being published is your aim, there's no point writing something that nobody wants to read.

Dan Brown certainly got the subject right with *The Da Vinci Code*, which sold more than 18 million copies worldwide and has been translated into forty-four languages. The book picked up on real history, mixed it with myth and presented it as a fictionalised story. Not only has that one book made Brown a multimillionaire (his earnings are reputed to be in the region of €200 million), it's the subject of guided tours in Paris, has spawned more than ten other works seeking to debunk it, has been made into a major motion picture and has been elevated to an evening course, titled 'Decoding Da Vinci', at Trinity College, Dublin.

Writing specifically to fill market requirements can also be a double-edged sword. While formulaic writing that appeases market requirements can make the bestseller list with its attendant huge advances and multiple translations, many writers want to be true to themselves and write from their heart.

When John Banville's *The Sea* won the 2005 Man Booker prize, he insisted in an interview in *The Sunday Times* that he would remain impervious to commercial considerations. 'I don't think any writer of any quality would allow himself to be affected in that way,' he said. 'When I was short-listed for the Booker last time around, I spent five years writing what was probably my most unsaleable book of all – *Ghosts*.'

Commercial versus true to self: that's a decision only you can make. Having said that, any of the big-earning writers I've heard speak about their work all have an enormous pride in their particular genre, be it chick lit, contemporary, crime fiction or literary. A careful tightrope has to be walked between intractability and the marketplace. There's little point in offering a subject the market doesn't want – unless you can find an original approach. So who determines what the markets want? That's a difficult question that's constantly changing, but is partly determined by agents, publishers and booksellers. The best advice is to write what you're passionate about, while at the same time keeping a weather eye on your genre. Avoid the temptation to write something you've no feeling for; such writing can, and frequently does, result in a sterile manuscript.

That said, there have been acres of newsprint, countless TV appearances and a lot of radio mileage given to the huge advances for the seemingly once-off, surprised-looking authors whose books make it to the bestseller lists. These are the rare phenomenon rather than the norm. Invariably and inevitably, a good book will out and not infrequently its author will have been quietly honing his or her craft over a considerable period of time.

THE BUSINESS OF WRITING

For the purpose of this book we're talking about the nuts and bolts of a business. Yes, a business. Writing – including novel writing – is like any other business. Between us writers, we know that to be published we'd crawl to Galway on our hands and knees, but that's a secret better not shared with publishers!

It's amazing to hear men and women who have been successful in their various walks of life come to writing a novel without an idea of its business implication. They make comments like, 'I don't mind if this book costs me', 'I hadn't thought of an advance', 'I'm not expecting a bestseller'. Worst of all is, 'It stays as I've written it, I won't make changes.'

One of the most important points about writing with the aim of publication is to realise that the publisher is in the business of making money and it doesn't bode well for you, as a writer, to approach them with 'novel preciousness', that amateur refusal to let go.

In other words, you're the writer. Only the writer. You write your first draft, and it's fine to do that with your heart. You then ensure your research is accurate, and using your head, you write and rewrite, revise and edit until you know this is as perfect as you can get your story.

Then and only then do you hand it over to your agent or publisher. It's their job to make editorial suggestions and yours, at this stage, to carry them out – not necessarily without dialogue, but remember, they're in the business of publishing and know what works within the pages of a novel. At this stage, a good agent will secure you a good deal and a good editor is your new best friend who can bring that final touch of magic to your novel.

But first, you have to write that novel.

In Stephen King's view, stories and novels consist of three parts: 'Narration which moves the story from point A to point

B and finally to point Z; description which creates a sensory reality for the reader; and dialogue which brings the characters to life through their speech.'

Think on that and read on...

PRELIMINARY WORK

It's frequently said that good fiction begins with the story and progresses to theme, that it seldom begins with theme and progresses to story.

You have your story idea for a novel. It's burning a hole in your heart, and your head is telling you to go for it. You sit at your laptop and start writing, the words flow as the characters leap into action and the plot unfolds miraculously, and all the time your creative juices flow. This is easy. You should have done it years ago.

For some lucky people this approach works, but usually, in their subconscious or at the back of their mind, they'll have had a good idea of characters, plot and often the ending and in all probability will have been mulling over their story for a considerable length of time.

Other writers who adopt this ad hoc approach can run out of creativity somewhere along the route of writing. Their characters lose their most appealing characteristics and become cardboard, their plot stalemates and they sit miserably, wondering what has gone wrong. Improvisation frequently runs out of steam.

For others, the stages of writing a novel are less dramatic, but more professional and attainable. Storyboarding can be of enormous benefit, though it's not a good idea to 'storyboard' a story to the exclusion of allowing yourself space for improvisation, to capture that magic moment when creativity is tooled by imagination.

STORYBOARDING

For storyboarding, many writers use white boards and markers in a variety of colours, though a jotter with large pages will do fine. The preliminary framework can run along the lines of:

- Main plot: Your primary storyline.
- Characters: The characters in your book (more about developing them later).
- Subsidiary plots: The secondary storylines, usually interweaving into the primary plot.

No matter how much storyboarding you do, it's important to bear in mind that there's no substitute for skill and technique, both of which come with experience, practice and determination. In the early stages, it's beneficial to have worked out the following:

- Genre: The category your novel falls into, e.g. thriller, crime novel, chick lit, historical. This often governs publicity and marketing.
- Theme: Simply what your story is about – adultery, domestic violence, childhood, etc.
- Locations: Where you place the action, whether at the races, in an A&E hospital ward, on a street in a specific city, etc.
- Time factor: The length of time your book spans. For instance, *Saturday* took place on a single Saturday in February, while the action in *The Time Traveller's Wife* occurred over more than half a century.
- Sequence of events: The order in which you relay your story to your reader. Even though it's likely the order will change during the first draft, not to mention during the rewrites, doing even a preliminary sequence at this stage helps focus.

Next we'll take a look at the pros and cons of detailed planning and that all-important synopsis.

PLANNING

In an interview with *The Sunday Times* after the publication of *Harry Potter and the Half Blood Prince*, J.K. Rowling said, 'I really planned the hell out of this. I took three months and just sat there and went over and over and over the plan, really fine-tuned it, looked at it from every angle.'

On the other hand, Roddy Doyle says:

> I never plan too meticulously. I read a novel years ago – I forget the title and author – about a writer who planned so carefully he could never work up the enthusiasm to actually write the books. It's good to have a general idea of the plot, or at least part of it, before starting. But I've learned to accept that a lot of the planning occurs while I'm writing, and that what seemed like good plot ideas go nowhere and end up in the bin. All stories are about characters. Can we ever know the characters well enough before writing to anticipate their every move and thought? I don't think so. I only began to really know my character, Paula Spencer, in *The Woman who Walked into Doors*, after the best part of a year of writing. I couldn't have 'planned' her. I had to write, to get to know her.

If you decide to go the planning route, write down anything relevant to the storyline, characters, plot development and location that comes to mind. If you're one of these people whose head is teeming with a variety of ideas, settle for one and stick to it. Try not to give in to the temptation of venturing down cul-de-sac plots. We can think anywhere: walking the dog, commuting to work, washing the dishes, disco dancing, playing a round of golf.

Characters

For each character, draw up a physical and psychological profile, note their age and name them. The act of naming is amazingly rewarding and breathes vitality and life into a character.

In this section I'm using my own work as an example because I can fully explain my thought sequences, how the story came together, the development of the various characters and, most importantly, the rewriting.

Before beginning to write my first novel, *Once Upon a Summer*, which was set in the summer of 1959, I knew the main character would be a teenage girl but initially I had difficulty naming her. Then one morning I woke up and knew she was called Rose, and during the day, from out of nowhere, Horn became her surname and slowly she came to life. She had short brown hair, wore a blue drindl skirt, was idealistic, loyal and a risk taker with a quirky sense of humour.

When her mother discovered Rose's secret trysts with Frank, she banished her to the depths of Kerry to stay with Cissie in the quiet seaside village of Fenit – far from temptation, she believed. Never did Mrs Horn suspect the sequence of events which would unfold.

While Rose and the other characters which peopled the novel were my creations to do with what I wished, I had to keep them consistent and ensure they acted in character throughout the chapters and yet underwent fictional metamorphosis.

Plot

Plot is hugely important. Quite simply, plot is the story, what happens in a book. In *Once Upon a Summer*, Rose befriends Mikey, who is the black sheep of the village, and is drawn into his life.

I knew from reading that the best plots are well paced, with some scenes fast and furious and full of drama, others slow and meandering, such as scenes of internal dialoguing. While battling to achieve this, I came to the slow realisation that in some obscure way, plot seemed to define structure.

Locations

At this stage, write down as much as you can, making a note of set pieces and locations. Look at the mileage Ian McEwan got out of a game of squash in *Saturday,* both moving plot forward and developing his main character.

If you're writing a murder scene, for example, you can optimise the drama by placing it in the right setting, using mood, atmosphere and ambience to their full potential. If there's a wedding in your novel, slip into the back of the church during a wedding ceremony and take copious notes. Well-done church scenes work extraordinarily well. Or how about setting one of your scenes at a race meeting? What a great excuse to attend the races – with notebook, of course. Again, capture the mood of a day – the horses, trainers, punters. Ask a few questions.

You don't have to travel to exotic places to come up with locations. Tune into the potential of your own area, looking at it through writing eyes. Make a map of streets, roads, houses, shops, churches, schools and other amenities. What types of shops sell what sorts of goods? What services are on offer? How would you describe your local community? There has to be a larger-than-life character somewhere – a boring know-all, a valuable historian, a loquacious drunk.

Most of us have done even a little travelling. Where have you been that's made an impression on you? It could be as holistic as a pilgrimage to the shrine at Knock or as hedonistic as a weekend at a wild rave in Ibiza.

As a writer, wherever you go, be aware of your surroundings. Who hasn't stepped off a plane in the Mediterranean to the heady fumes of heat and diesel and wafts of that potent cologne so beloved of Continental men? Who hasn't strolled through country markets with their stalls laden with cheeses, brown soda bread and fresh apple juice? Who hasn't been to a funeral service, listened to the priest or clergyman extol the dead, watched the body language of the grieving family, seen the different mannerisms of people offering their condolences? Such experiences and sequences are grist to the mill of a writer.

We're surrounded by the potential of set pieces and locations the minute we step out our hall door – even before. There's nothing to stop us using descriptions of our own house or apartment in our writing.

Get all or some of the above down in some shape or form – notes, bullet points, phrases, words focusing on characters, plot lines, locations and anything else pertinent to your burgeoning novel. Some writers use whiteboards and markers throughout; others jot things down in a notebook; some key it in tidily with appropriate tabs, stars and underlining; while others stick bits of paper around the place with ideas, jottings, touches of characteristics and thoughts on plots. It's the doing, not the how you do it, that matters.

Have you got a title yet? Some authors use their title as a starting point; others know a word or phrase will present itself during the course of their writing which will become the title; some write using a working title; while others label their work Book1. As I write, I'm calling this BIP8, which stands for book in progress and it's my eighth.

A title is of vital importance, but it's not something to worry about if one doesn't present itself to you. The marketing person or publicist in your publishing company will be happy to lend a hand. Even if you have what you consider to be the most thrilling title, your publisher may decide otherwise.

SYNOPSIS

While established writers use a synopsis as a tool to let a publisher know about their as-yet-unwritten novel, it can help beginners to further organise their thoughts. A synopsis should show that you know:

- What you're writing about.
- Who your characters are.
- The market you're writing for.
- How to present an analysis of a story not yet written.

It helps to break down a synopsis as follows:

- Introduction: A statement of between five and fifteen lines written in the style of a back cover blurb, highlighting the most significant selling points.
- Character biographies: Short biographies of all the major characters. It's essential to make clear who the main character is and what motivates him or her. (Yes, I know, you've already done characters, but not in the context of a synopsis.)
- Storyline: This should be a relatively brief description of the story of your novel; between five and ten pages works well. This is difficult to write in detail at this stage and it is inevitable and understood by publishers that you will make changes – though nothing radical without checking first with them or your agent.

Now you're ready to begin the process of real writing. In the following sections we'll be dealing with topics such as the first draft, researching, rewriting, editing and revising and presentation.

WRITING A NOVEL

First Draft

When you've done the preliminary work, now is the time to begin writing.

Once started, the perceived wisdom at this stage is to write and keep writing without going into reverse for editing. But, again, that's up to the individual. Several professional writers admit to getting some way into the book before doing an about turn to edit. Others – frequently those who use detailed advance planning and plotting – can go from beginning to end.

Many professional writers say that once they start work on a project, they don't stop unless they absolutely have to. They find that if they don't write every day, their characters become blurred and no longer seem like real people. Worst of all the excitement of creating something new drifts away.

A first draft is usually written from the heart. Our initial writing is telling ourselves the story, whereas rewriting, editing, revision – call it what you will – is done for our readers, and needs to be organised from the head.

Again, it's important to reiterate that there are no hard and fast rules. Remember at this stage we are only talking draft. As you write, more than likely new ideas, refinements on characters and further enhancements of plot will clamour for inclusion. Do listen to your heart – give your characters their head and allow them to romp through changes, though try to keep them within character and within the framework of the main plot.

Sometimes in the most unlikely situation a stream of consciousness presents itself, flowing and rippling in perfection. Go with it. Such bounty doesn't often happen when writing. At the worst, you can edit it out later.

'How long should a chapter be?' is a frequently asked question. They can be as long or as short as the story demands.

However, there's something disconcerting about a novel with wildly uneven chapter sizes, which can become an obstacle to readers' enjoyment. But equally, a novel with rigid metrical chapters can also be a distraction.

Many people believe that if only they had the time, they'd write a bestseller. Perhaps that's true, though from experience I've learned that people who are passionate about wanting to write, no matter how busy, will make the time to write.

Sunday evenings is when Tom Bradby, political editor of *ITV News*, writes his novels, assisted in plotting and characterisation by his jewellery-designer wife Claudia. Maeve Binchy has been known to suggest that people strapped for time with demanding jobs and/or children write, say, 2,000 words on a Saturday and 3,000 words on Sunday, giving them 5,000 words a week. For those who make – note the verb 'make' – the opportunity to write 1,000 words daily – about four pages of double spaced A4 paper – your first draft should be achievable without too much effort, particularly if you've done some planning.

Stephen King believes the first draft of a book should take no longer than three months – 'the length of a season'. He writes 2,000 words a day. Some days, he says, his pages come easily; other days they're harder to achieve.

Other writers find that assigning themselves blocks of pre-ordained hours for writing works for them – research shows that our attention span somewhat depletes after two hours of concentration. A cautionary word here: as already pointed out, making a coffee or ringing a friend is not writing, and has no place within that two-hour framework.

While our writing is as individual as our fingerprints, our modus operandi is equally individual. There's nothing written in stone about the way we should manage our writing time. What works for one writer may not work for another and vice versa. We usually arrive at a working format by trial and error. Again, it's a matter of finding your own level, what best suits you and your lifestyle. It's difficult to put life on permanent hold for the length of time it takes to write and edit a novel. It's much easier to do so for the requisite days or weeks required when working on features or short stories.

At book signings, a regular question is 'Do you handwrite or use a computer?' To date there has been no qualitative survey into the effects of electronic cut-and-pasting on literary style. If you're handwriting, the movement of thought tends to be linear, accretive, from one sentence to the next. Writers used to write in series. The writer using a word processor can, effectively, write in parallel.

'I write direct onto a laptop,' says Roddy Doyle. 'I've haven't used longhand in years. I'm much happier typing. Editing is so much easier.'

As you progress with your writing, discipline becomes the key word. It has rightly been said that writing is more perspiration than creation. Like the start of a love affair, it's heady and exciting in the beginning – you can't wait to revisit your story, to reacquaint yourself with your characters – but at some stage, like the best of love affairs, the wonder becomes the ordinary and a sensation of monotony sets in.

This is the stage that separates the wannabes from the professionals. Now is the time that you assiduously do that two hours, write that 1,000 words – one letter after another until you have a word, several words later you have a sentence, then a paragraph and finally a page. Even though your words may appear leaden on the page when you're in a slog mindset, they can be edited to dynamism later.

Congratulations! You've completed your first draft. And it does call for celebration, even a little break from writing. Some gurus maintain that at this point writers need to separate themselves both geographically and psychologically from their writing. Remember William Trevor putting his writing in a drawer for a year and then taking it out for reworking? And by the way, he handwrites. As did the late John McGahern, author of six highly acclaimed novels and four collections of short stories, and considered by literary reviewers to have been one of the finest writers working in prose.

Research

In the course of her research, crime writer Patricia Cornwell has learned to fly a helicopter, mastered a Harley Davidson and subjected herself to a brain scan to ascertain the difference between the criminal and non-criminal mind.

Most research doesn't entail quite as much bravado. When American writer Rick Moody decided to open his latest novel *The Diviners* with a description of light throughout the universe, he bought a globe and some dental floss which he taped to Los Angeles, then wrapped it around the globe so that he had an axis to use as a leaping-off point. Once he had that, wherever he was on the globe, he would pick four or five locations to explore further.

After you've written your first draft can be a good time to do fine-tooth-comb research. Now, you say? Surely research should be done before starting writing? If you're writing non-fiction, then the answer is definitely yes. If you're writing fiction, the answer is both yes and no. Obviously if your book is set in Australia and you've never been there, you'll have to carry out research before you start writing, or if you're setting your novel in Victorian London, you need to be familiar with your subject.

But for the like of dates that crop up, points that need clarification, music of the time, food of the era, clothes and so on, they can all be dropped at this stage. By doing this:
- You haven't slowed down the plot with research which can make a novel top-heavy. I've heard a description that the perfect usage of research is rather like chewing the cud, which the cow spits out once it has absorbed the nutrients.
- You'll be less inclined to write factually. One of the secrets of good fiction is to show, not tell.

'I read as I write, if I need to do formal research, I'm open to going back and adding an image or fact to something already written, if I come across something interesting as I read,' says Roddy Doyle.

I wrote a book set in New York in the '20s. I started writing before I started doing research. This, I think, helped me concentrate more on the research. I was looking for images, impressions, that would give sharpness to the writing. It also helped with the plot. I saw a photograph of a sandwich board man, by Sam Fuller. I gave my narrator that job. I was wondering what the narrator would do for a living as I was flicking through the photographs. I'm not sure I'd have noticed the sandwich board if I hadn't been thinking about possible jobs for Henry, the narrator.

Doyle believes in visiting known locations.

Sometimes it's useful to visit places you intend writing about. When I was writing *Paddy Clarke Ha Ha Ha*, I went to my parents' house, where I grew up. The kitchen is basically as it was when I was a child; different utensils etc. and paint, but it's the same shape. I got down on my knees, so I could look around as a much smaller person, a kid, would. This helped. I could look at the fridge from a kid's angle.

When I was writing *A Star Called Henry*, part of which is set in the GPO in Dublin, I went into the GPO, but that was no real help. I found it impossible to imagine that anything dramatic had ever happened there. Books were much more useful in that case. And that went for Dublin generally, in the early 20th century. Books such as Joyce's *Dubliners* are more useful than walking around contemporary Dublin.

My book, *Oh Play That Thing*, is set in New York and Chicago. Walking around the Lower East Side of Manhattan was great; structurally it hasn't changed that much. It was easy to visualise my characters walking those streets. A trip to the South Side of Chicago, though, wasn't as beneficial. The streets that Louis Armstrong walked and that Richard Wright wrote about in, for example, *Native Son* have been demolished. Only one original jazz club still stands. All the other buildings are gone. But, then, that one remaining building, now a hardware store, was well worth the visit. The original stage is hidden at the back of the shop. I stood on the stage. Armstrong stood there. Duke Ellington played there. It was actually very small. This was a huge help when I started writing about the life of the clubs.

EDITING, REWRITING, REVISING

The word 'revision' is derived from the Latin *'revisere'*, 'to see again'. Revision is the opportunity we give ourselves, as writers, 'to see it again' more fully, more richly, more deeply, more meaningfully.

Rewriting, editing and revising fall into three main categories:

- Revising for structure: This ensures your story is told in the most coherent and dramatically effective way. The main problems that need to be dealt with here are:
  - ~ Lack of dramatisation in the story.
  - ~ Overwriting or underwriting scenes.
  - ~ Unnecessary characters and action.
  - ~ Out-of-sequence narrative events.
  - ~ Weak openings and endings.
- Revising for meaning: Makes certain that the words you write convey precisely what you want to say. The basic rule of vocabulary is to use the first word that comes to mind, if it's appropriate and colourful. If you hesitate and think, you'll come up with another word – of course you will, there are always several other words – but likely none of them will be as good as your first choice, or as close to what you really mean.
- Revising for style: This is about telling your story in a beautifully crafted way, which is often all beginning writers consider revision to be.

While revising for structure, meaning and style there are several additional pointers to look for, listed below.

Point of Entry

Is your point of entry right? Firstly, it has to whet your publisher's appetite to read on. Secondly, after perusing the cover and reading back cover blurbs, most would-be book buyers read the first few sentences of the book. Will yours ensure they want to read on – in other words, buy your book? Point of entry should grab attention.

Note the opening sentence of Salman Rushdie's multi-award-winning *Midnight's Children*: 'I was born in the city of Bombay...once upon a time.' Or consider the opening sentence of international bestseller *The Shadow of the Wind* by Carlos Ruiz Zafón: 'I still remember the day my father took me to the Cemetery of Forgotten Books for the first time.' J.K. Rowling's *Harry Potter and the Order of the Phoenix* begins, 'The hottest day of the summer so far was drawing to a close and a drowsy silence lay over the large square houses of Privet Drive.' June Considine opens her second adult novel, *Deceptions*, simply with, 'Dublin is a city with eyes.'

They are different books, different genres and different styles but with one thing in common – they all open with hook sentences that lead into the perfect point of entry.

Showing Rather than Telling

Throughout your novel, have you shown rather than told? Many new writers are inclined to tell the story without showing the various sequences. It's an easy trap to fall into and can often be avoided by employing the senses. Use your eyes, ears and senses of taste, smell and touch.

Viewpoint Character(s) Voice

Is your story told in the correct voice or voices? All the way through, have you used the right viewpoint character? A book's voice can be written in several ways:
- Overview or third person, as in the Harry Potter books, allows the author to get on objectively with telling the story.
- One-dimensional, through the eyes of the main character works well with a strong character and a strongly focused story. Who can forget Paula in Roddy Doyle's *The Woman*

who Walked into Doors or Christine Dwyer Hickey's poignant Tatty in the novel of the same title.

- Multi-dimensional, the story told through the voices of the various characters allows readers to dip into the lives of the various characters. It is said to have been pioneered by Jack Higgins of *The Eagle has Landed* fame and is attractive to movie and television producers, as it allows for easier adaptation of material from print to screen.
- First person, as in *The Shadow of the Wind* by Spanish writer Carlos Ruiz Zafón. First person gives an intimacy to writing.

There are no golden rules, no right or wrong way of writing viewpoint character, though readers should be able to identify with him or her.

Characters

Ensure that your characters, whether they're mousey or dynamic, make a grand entrance rather than crawling into your book under the carpet. A ploy that works well is to introduce your character's physical and psychological characteristics gradually – gradual introduction works wonderfully for forwarding plot.

Rose is introduced in Chapter 1 of *Once Upon a Summer* wondering if she should tell her best friends that there's a boy she really fancies. "'There's this boy…" she began hesitantly, a soft smile lighting up her heart-shaped face.' Throughout your manuscript, ensure your characters act in character – while undergoing her metamorphosis, Rose kept her integrity and didn't change physically – sapphire blue eyes didn't become green halfway through the novel.

Plot and Structure

Plot is simply the telling of your story, and structure is how you go about constructing your story. Remember, plot begins when a problem occurs that requires a reaction from one of your characters. Plot must have structure and, as mentioned earlier, pace. Plot needs to forward the storyline at the pace of the book – for instance, a murder scene is best not followed by a horrific car crash, or a domestic kitchen scene may have more impact if it's separated from a claustrophobic family dinner. Plot also needs pace. It's said that pace is to fiction what buses are to commuters – regular arrival, neither too many or too few.

The first draft of *Once Upon a Summer* took me most of a year to edit to publishable standard. To get rid of all those out-of-sequence events which peppered my first drafts, I restructured and tightened the whole book.

On about my fifth rewrite to create more drama in the last third of the book, I inserted the scene where Mikey is in the car crash that kills his parents; initially, I overwrote the 'rosary at night' scene and spent a long time cutting it to appropriate size; I underwrote the circumstances in which Cissie became pregnant; I reduced Cissies's friends from four to two and pared back several action scenes which were taking away from the primary storyline.

Finally, to give the book a modern touch which I hoped might give it more purchase appeal, I opened with a prologue set in modern times, which introduced the main characters and hinted at the plot, and ended with a bracketing epilogue.

Revision is fun, particularly revision of fiction. It's imaginative play with no referees, no critics, just you and your story. No one is counting. No one is rushing you – unless you're working to a deadline. You're free, you can try anything and everything and you get as many chances and can take as long as you want to make it perfect.

To succeed, the majority of writers need a devotion to revision, to a merciless reworking of their work until it's the best it can be, stylistically, conceptually and dramatically. Talent and craft will only take you so far. If a writer is content with his first draft, the world will know it; if content with the next draft, his fellow writers will know; if content with one almost perfect except for a few glitches, perhaps, with luck, only he will know it.

Roddy Doyle says:

> I edit every day. I start each day by going over what I did the previous day, and sometimes further back. I like the story to be in good shape as I progress – not too rough – but I accept that there are times when it isn't flowing well, and I just continue through it in the knowledge that I'll go back later and do a very strict edit. Put simply, it's sometimes necessary to write five dull sentences to get to the one you actually want. But it's important to recognise the five dull ones, and get rid of them.

It's in revision that good fiction is made. Only in fiction do stories fall perfect from your imagination to pen to paper! The purpose of writing a story is to *rewrite* it. The purpose of the first draft is to get us to the second; the purpose of the second is to get us to the third; the third to the fourth and on and on.

Tolstoy wrote and rewrote *War and Peace* eight times; Frank O'Connor, Irish short story maestro, said he revised endlessly, endlessly, endlessly. French novelist Colette said that anyone can write down anything that comes into their heads, 'but an author is one who can judge his stuff's worth, without pity and destroy most of it.' It's a paradox of writing that this 'destruction' is mostly a creation.

Revising, rewriting and editing is a glorious stage – not necessarily easy, but certainly glorious. You have your plot and characters, you've told your story. Now all that remains is to improve on it. If you don't yet have the perfect title, now is the time to look out for a hinge phrase within your book. An avid reader friend of mind loves spotting appropriate titles within pages.

Only when your book is pruned or amplified, as necessary, and rewritten and edited to your level of perfection, is it time to send it off to an agent or publisher, not before. A good rule of thumb is never to let anything you've written out of your hand before it's as perfect as you can make it.

6

writing
for
children

'The stars through the window pane are my children.' John Keats

A rule of thumb when writing for children is never to under-estimate either their knowledge or their intelligence. Language is crucial: word play, repetition and rhythm are all important. Children need stories that tap into their effective concerns, their fears and desires, as well as being a good read. The same rules that apply to adult fiction are also relevant when writing for children:

• Good plot.
• Credible characters.
• Authentic locations.

Around 44 million children's books are sold in Britain annually, an increase of 9 million over the past five years. We don't have a similar statistic for Ireland, but taking into account our reputation as a nation of readers, per capita it's generally conceded to be approximately the same, if not more.

Children's fiction is big business, yet the myth persists that children's books are easy to write: every year, each of the big English publishers receives in the region of 5,000 unsolicited children's books. Of these, only between 1 and 2 per cent make it into print. Writers that do succeed invariably use language well and have the ability to create a narrative intimacy with a young audience.

In publishing circles, much is made of the current renaissance of children's writing, which readily translates into the phenomenon that is J.K. Rowling's Harry Potter series, which has become a crossover classic. Another book that started out exclusively for children and was hijacked by adults is Mark Hadden's *The Curious Incident of the Dog in the Nighttime*. Jumping on this crossover bandwagon, Faber & Faber, in con-junction with Waterstones, launched a Wow Factor search for the new J.K. Rowling, and *Saga* magazine and HarperCollins have started a hunt for a new writing talent in the 50-plus age bracket under the banner 'Are you the next J.K. Rowling?'

Michael O'Brien of The O'Brien Press, whose name is widely known as a publisher of children's books in Ireland, lists the ten commandments of writing for children:

- Remember there is a huge range of books for children – fiction, information books, humour, history, biography, etc. Work to your strengths.
- A good publisher will recognise talent even if the story is flawed. Good writing comes first (and second and third!). Dump text that you know in your heart won't work.
- Work out THE IDEA for the book first – it can be magical, contemporary, humorous, adventure, nature, futuristic, factual, whatever. The more distinctive, the better the chance of success.
- Think of children of a particular reading age – a big market is for ages seven to nine, but it seems to be the most challenging. Write for the age you are comfortable with.
- Sometimes writing for children is seen as an easy option – not so. Children are harsh critics, and for readers under nine years of age the parents and other adults have a big say in book purchases.
- Remember – the story comes first, so don't fuss about illustrations (unless you're a skilled illustrator).
- Don't necessarily trust the opinion of your relations or of children you have read aloud to.
- If *you* are not happy with your story, then it will disappoint a publisher too.
- Good children's fiction stays in print for many years and can reach a huge international translation market. (O'Brien Press has hundreds of books published in translation in dozens of languages worldwide.)
- Think about a publisher's reputation – awards, range of titles and series, standards of design, editing, marketing, distribution and international representation. This can work wonders for your work.

Award-winning writer Siobhán Parkinson wrote her first children's book for her son when he was six. She says, 'It just sort of...happened.'

When people ask her what she does for a living, she says she's a writer, but when she adds, 'Mainly for children, I watch the sudden spark of interest that flared with the "I'm a writer" die right in front of my eyes. Or else there's the sudden gush of, "How lovely!" It's quite funny, actually.'

It's not 'lovely' to write for children just because they are children. It's a genre you write within, like any other, with its own demands and constraints, and it's a permanent challenge. It's like doing really hard crosswords all the time, always trying to figure out how you're going to solve something. (This is in the nature of writing, not in the nature of writing for a particular age group, by the way.) And like doing really hard crosswords, it's not just hard but satisfying. But it's not 'lovely', it's not as if you are the tooth fairy or anything.

Parkinson doesn't see being a children's writer as all that specialised:

It's really just writing. Writing is the thing, using language. That's the task, and that's the pleasure. The audience is important, but you aren't writing to the audience as you sit down every day. You just write. You keep the audience in mind in so far as you have to think, Would a reader want to read this? Will a reader be convinced by this? As soon as you think, Maybe not, then you ditch that bit – you keep a sort of theoretical reader in mind all right, to keep you on track, to prevent yourself slipping into self-indulgence.

If you thought about your actual audience, you'd never write anything. You write for yourself, but not in a self-indulgent way (or not if you expect to be read), you write for the reader you are, not for the person you are. That's it, the reader in yourself is your first audience, and the audience you have to convince.

If you write for children, then the reader in yourself that you write for is yourself as a child reader, your eleven-year-old self. Even if it's a very long time since you've been eleven, she's still in there, and she still has a shit-detector. The shit-detector improves, actually, so she's harder and harder to write for.

Parkinson has written across the ages, but says her real 'home' as a writer is the ten to twelve age group.

> That's because at this age, children are no longer, by and large, still struggling with the reading process, deciphering text word by word. They are really reading like adults, fluently, engaging with characters, and are ready for anything. I don't mean you just fling any old thing at them, or that you expect to engage them with what will engage an adult, but they are to be respected as a readership, they are smart, they are so much smarter than adults suspect, and truly almost any subject is suitable, as long as it is appropriately handled. And yet they still have that ability to enter the world of the book with complete passion and abandon, an ability that adults have lost. So, they are ideal readers.

Recognition is also important to Parkinson.

> One person saying, I loved this book, it made me laugh/cry, it made me want to go on reading. That's more like it. I approve of awards, because they (sometimes) direct readers towards outstanding books, but for that swelling feeling of oh, YES, I've done it – it's

the individual you meet who looks at you with shining eyes, and says, I loved it! And better still is the reader who can say, I loved it because... That's a writer's reader. That's a highlight.

TIPS ON WRITING FOR CHILDREN

'Write. Write. Write. That's all. Except also, read, read, read. And think, think, think. I don't know what else to advise,' says Siobhán Parkinson. 'It's not easy, but writing is enjoyable.'

She says there are two points that must not be underestimated:

- The audience. They are as intelligent as you are, or they wouldn't want to read your work, and you shouldn't want them to, either, because what's the value of writing to a less intelligent audience than yourself?
- The work involved in writing.

'Sure, if you are practised and reasonably good with words, you can churn stuff out. But churning stuff out won't do your self-respect any good. To retain your self-respect, you need to write the best you can, and that comes back to think, think, think, read, read, read and write, write, write. Edit, edit, edit is quite good too,' is the advice from Siobhán Parkinson, who says she doesn't have a favourite part of writing. 'I just do it. I enjoy it all. I like working, that's all. I edit as I write and write as I edit.'

7

non-fiction

'It's a fact the whole world knows,
That Pobbles are happier without their toes.' Edward Lear

ANALYSING YOUR IDEA

Before pitching, think further. Is your idea plump rather than thin? No pun intended, but the wealth of books on food, wine, dieting and cooking are all plump.

Will it be of value to the reader? The most successful travel books, such as Michael Palin's *Himalaya*, in addition to being attractive to the eye and interesting to browse through, offer an amount of valuable information and a dream that appears to be achievable to the masses as well.

As well as being about something, non-fiction books work better if they have a clearly defined purpose. For example, this book is aimed at writers at a variety of stages in their writing.

Who will buy your book? Who will read it? Visualise your market. If you can't do this, you're less likely to sell your idea to a publisher.

Is your book topical? In non-fiction, immediacy and topicality are an advantage. Note the rash of books in 2005 commemorating Horatio Nelson and the 200-year anniversary of the Battle of Trafalgar, the sixtieth anniversary of the dropping of the first atom bomb or the number of biographies timed to commemorate the birth of Hans Christian Andersen in 1805. In 2006, the market was flooded with an avalanche of Mozart literature published to coincide with the composer's 250th birthday.

Is your idea original or are you putting an original spin on a well-proven topic? In the world of writing, different is good. You have a better chance of being taken on by a publisher if your book is somehow unique. For instance, consider Dean Karnazes's *Ultramarathon Man: Confessions of an All-Night Runner*, charting his passion for running ultramarathons, races of a minimum of fifty miles. It became an unexpected bestseller in the US, and Karnazes was swarmed at book signings to which, of course, he ran. *To See Every Bird on Earth* by Dan Koeppel is another unlikely subject.

The market for non-fiction is insatiable. Think of the number of cookery books that are not only published but bought, as well as gardening books, travel books, self-help books, how-to books, not to mention autobiographies, biographies, memoirs, histories and sport. And there's money to be made, too. English footballer Wayne Rooney made sports writing publishing history with his £5 million book deal.

Recently we have witnessed the rise in popularity of what's being called 'biographical fiction', which is exactly what it sounds like – a biography of someone with a dash of fiction. *Matisse the Master*, the biography of French painter Henri Matisse by English author Hilary Spurling, is a prime example. It went on to win the 2006 Whitbread Book of the Year Award. Interestingly, when Spurling began her research, she discovered that what little there was on record about Matisse was of dubious origin and veracity.

The good news for writers is that it's easier to sell an idea for a non-fiction book to a publisher than it is to sell a completed work of fiction. Publishers buy non-fiction more readily than fiction, mainly because it has a more clearly defined market niche and it's more straightforward for their marketing department to influence the final shape of the book.

Being able to sell on your idea or even to have your idea favourably considered brings freedom of mind and allows you to get on with the business of research, interviewing, drafting and writing without gambling months or even years on what may turn out to be an unsaleable book.

An idea that's marketable and fills a gap in the book-buying market is the essential component for a non-fiction book. If you have an idea that hasn't been overworked or overdone – it's too much to hope that you've come up with a virgin idea – all the better. Lucky you. While the fate of a book, particularly a non-fiction book, depends on many factors, without a good idea, well executed, it will never be born.

Mary Kenny's non-fiction works include a cultural history of Ireland called *Goodbye to Catholic Ireland* (London 1997 and Dublin 2000). She says that this entailed looking at the social and cultural values over the space of her parents' lives (from the death of Parnell to the rise of Mary Robinson). She has also written a short book about heroin addiction, as well as *Germany Calling*, the biography of Lord Haw-Haw. In 2004 she self-published, *Allegiance*, a play about the relationship between Winston Churchill and Michael Collins. Currently she is working on a new book with an Anglo-Irish theme and a contemporary twenty-first-century twist.

Kenny says:

> You need an interesting, marketable idea (I had an engaging book idea in 2004, but it didn't turn out to be marketable), accessible research and, I'm afraid, increasingly, good (or even bad) publicity. We live in a very media-aware and celebrity-aware culture, which has its downside: I have come across cases of writers having their work turned down on the grounds that they were too old, too unattractive or too unprepossessing to be 'marketed'. The bookselling trade today is also full of hype and bullshit, as it has been taken over by monopolies and conglomerates which push titles they consider sexy and marketable, and often ignore real merit.
>
> Yet persistence overcomes all obstacles, in the end, and that is essential for any aspiring writer. Persist and persist and persist again. Many books which afterwards found a lasting readership were turned down repeatedly by publishers, so you have to believe in yourself. If you can get a good agent, it helps: but good agents are like hen's teeth and there is an extraordinary dearth of agents in Ireland.

What happens next when you have this g
have to develop it in a way that will attrac
remembering that it's your same idea that wi
book is stocked (hopefully in a prominent pl
sellers), will attract media coverage, be reviewed
the book-buying public that they should not on
copy in the bookshop, scan the front cover, re
cover blurb, glance at the contents, study the o
flick through the pages, but actually buy it.

Pitching your idea is where a professional app
dividends. Many a feasible idea has been shot down
lisher because of a sloppy, ill-researched presentatio

It's the story of his father's passion for bird-watching and identification of the approximately 9,600 bird species on earth.

Is your idea possible? Possible is essential. When you make your pitch, the publisher must believe that you can research, write and market it.

A MARKETABLE BOOK

As well as your golden idea and dynamic pitch, you must be confident of your ability to produce the book, either because you're already familiar with the subject or because you know your research routes.

Up to now, when talking about non-fiction we've presumed you're blessed with a brilliantly marketable idea. But what if you're casting around for that elusive idea? Would like to write non-fiction but aren't sure what to write about? Try asking yourself the following questions.

- What information do I have that I would be interested in writing about? Would people be interested?
- What subject would I be passionately interested in researching?

The first category might cover existing work skills, a hobby or a personal experience, such as Dean Karnazes running ultra-marathons, which he mostly dictated into a recorder as he ran.

Nigella Lawson began cooking at the encouragement of her first husband and now, as well as becoming a seriously rich woman, has brought a sexual trendiness into cooking. Jamie Oliver started out as a cook with attitude and passion and ended up changing people's attitudes to school food in Britain, during which process he became a cult figure. In a more homely vein, Darina Allen's and Jenny Bristow's cookbooks are prime examples of using existing skills to utmost benefit. They have both honed their natural ability, experience and lifestyle to write books that tie into their television programmes, cooking weekends, seminars and lectures.

It's a well-proven fact that the general public are interested in anything to do with achievement. The unknown and human endeavour is always interesting. When he reached the 7,000 mark for sightings of birds, Richard Koeppel became one of only twelve such birders in the world. Lifestyle backed with personal experience is also a sure-fire winner.

Or note the success of Trinny Woodall and Susannah Constantine's *What Not to Wear* manual, again tied into their television series. Both the book and the series have become big in the US. Interestingly, Susannah started her career in journalism reporting on cricket matches.

Diet books are always popular, though to write a successful one, it helps either to be a celebrity or to have credibility, like a proven success rate, such as being the instigator of the Atkins Diet or GI diets, or keeping it personal, like losing six stone in four months!

If you're going to research and write a book that will take months of work, you need to enjoy your subject, even if you started out on non-fiction casting around for a marketable idea. If you're writing only because you think there might be a market and the subject doesn't particularly appeal to you, you'll have a miserable time researching and writing and chances are it will be reflected in the finished product.

SUSSING OUT THE MARKET

The first stage in writing a non-fiction book is to suss out the market. Browse around the non-fiction shelves of several of the bigger bookshops and see who's publishing the type of book you plan to write. For this, we're staying within the Irish market. By examining the various books, you'll get a better feel of the market than using a reference book. But when you've more or less settled on one or two publishers, by all means look up the company in the *Writers' & Artists' Yearbook* or the *Writers' Handbook*, both of which are bibles of information for writers and are updated annually.

CONTACTING THE PUBLISHER

In Chapter 8, you'll find a list of the publishers in the North and South of Ireland, and if you decide to look for an agent, you'll find the few Irish agents listed; follow their guidelines for submission.

If you're an established writer or a writer whose name will be known to the publisher, you can make a phone call, ask for a minute of the publisher's time and run the subject matter and basic outline of your idea by him or her. At this stage you're just looking for approval in principle, and if they're interested you can follow it up either with a meeting or with a detailed outline of your proposal.

If you're a beginner, I suggest you write a letter – yes, snail mail. Publishers are busy and may be irritated rather than interested if disturbed by a phone call from someone they don't know, and unexpected pitches from unknown writers can get lost in the daily spate of junk e-mails. Book publishing doesn't usually have the immediacy of newspaper and magazine journalism, so it's not a case of a story going cold.

Keep your letter as brief as possible. Remember, a good idea well pitched leaps out at a publisher. All you need to include at this stage is:

- Your proposed subject.
- Who you are and your suitability to write on your subject.
- The basic idea of your book stated in one sentence.
- Make it clear why your book is original or at least different from other books on the subject.
- List potential readers and why they will buy this book.
- Provide details on structure, e.g. live interviews, photographs.
- Give facts and statistics.
- Offer to supply a detailed treatment and/or sample chapters.

MAKING YOUR PITCH

If the publisher is interested, he'll ask you to provide the more detailed treatment and sample chapters, which ideally should be the first and second and, if necessary, one other chapter. Each publishing house has its own requirements and it creates a professional impression if you ask what they are and adhere to them.

For example, editor Brian Langan of The Liffey Press says, 'We look to publish high-quality non-fiction books of Irish interest. Recent titles include Carole Coleman's *Alleluia America!*, Joe Humphreys's *The Story of Virtue*, Bruce Arnold's *The Spire and Other Essays on Modern Irish Culture* and John Waters's *The Politburo Has Decided That You Are Unwell.*'

The requirements for writers approaching The Liffey Press are:

- A brief proposal outlining the theme, argument or idea behind your book.
- A synopsis of 100-200 words.
- A proposed list of contents.
- What sort of market/audience you hope to reach.
- Details of competing titles, if any.
- Short biographical note (50 words) about yourself.
- Introductory chapter and/or one or two sample chapters (or 30-50 pages).

'Proposals can be sent by e-mail or post,' says Langan. 'We try to respond promptly, but at busy times of the year, a reply can take three or four weeks.'

From your treatment and chapters, the publisher should be able to judge the focus and direction of your work as well as your ability to research and analyse, your knowledge of the subject and your command of language. The treatment should be between six and ten double-spaced pages in length and provide detail on research sources.

Your pitch may convince the publisher that your proposed

project is promising, at which point you may be offered a contract or asked to provide further chapters. Go for it! You now know that your idea is sound and commercially viable. Equally important, the publisher is giving you a chance and is obviously willing to work with you.

With more leisure time, disposable income and increased emphasis on adult education, which for the past two decades is on a continuous growth curve, people are actively seeking to acquire knowledge and to learn new skills. Note the expansion and variation of the Adult Education Courses being facilitated by UCD, UCC, UCG, Ulster University and Magill University, and the comprehensive programme of learning for adults put out by the various Colleges of Further Education. As well as courses catering for this craving for knowledge, there has been an increase in the number of books published on the various subjects.

People whose speciality wouldn't have seen the light of day beyond their own homes a decade ago can, if they so wish, detail their skills into books. Have you seen the number of books on embroidery, woodwork and stone walls?

For many people, their career speciality becomes a bestselling, marketable skill. Eamon Dunphy turned his league soccer time into journalism, being a chat show host and biography writer. When broadcaster Lynne Truss, who is passionate about grammar, wrote *Eats, Shoots & Leaves* based on her BBC Radio 4 programmes, it became an instant success.

RESEARCHING AND GATHERING INFORMATION

Dan Koeppel says that while writing *To See Every Bird on Earth*, he accumulated hundreds of pages of transcribed interviews with his father. As inevitably happens with interviews and compiling information, some sessions were fun, others tedious, some painful. But as every writer of successful nonfiction knows, every last research stone must be upturned.

BIOGRAPHY, AUTOBIOGRAPHY AND MEMOIR

The market for autobiographies, biographies and memoirs of popular, controversial, celebrity or colourful figures is constantly growing. Time was when autobiographies were penned by internationally renowned figures in their twilight years with a wealth of success behind them. No more.

For example, take *Geldof in Africa* by indefatigable human rights campaigner Bob Geldof; thirty-something Jools Oliver, wife of school-dinner activist Jamie, getting in on the act with *Minus Nine to One*, a diary of her experiences of motherhood; not to mention *Being Jordan* by Katie Price, the tabloids' favourite glamour model. And then there's *Gazza: My Story* by Paul Gascoigne, written with help from Hunter Davies, all of which resided in the UK bestseller list for several months.

Nearly a decade on from her death, Princess Diana is still a source of rich pickings for biographers. David Beckham and his wife, former Spice Girl Victoria, only barely in their thirties, are also the subject of several biographies.

Flagged as one of the biographies of the decade is *Mao: The Unknown Story* by Jung Chang, author of perennial bestseller *Wild Swans*, and her historian husband, Jon Halliday. It's a heavily researched work and turns many of the popular Western perceptions about Mao on their head. The fact that it was banned on mainland China has only added to its popularity.

There are two schools of thought on whether 'authorised' or 'unauthorised' is the purest form of biography. Publishers use both words as positive selling points from different angles. The authorised biography has the blessing of the subject, which suggests the author has more information than would have been available to an unauthorised biographer. On the other hand, it can seem that the subject had a strong say in what can and can't be included. The book can therefore appear censored.

The unauthorised biography suggests either that the subject did not consider the writer sufficiently important to merit their time, or that there is something in the book they would prefer to suppress. It can also imply that a book has been hastily put together from a collection of newspaper and magazine features, radio and television interviews to cash in on a sudden surge in the subject's popularity. High-profile people often withhold co-operation from biographers because they plan to write their own story.

Probably the greatest memoir success story of recent times is *Angela's Ashes*, written by Frank McCourt at the age of sixty when he retired from teaching in New York and started, as he describes it, 'scribbling'. *Angela's Ashes*, which tells of his childhood in Limerick, went into *The New York Times* bestseller list, made him rich and famous and earned McCourt the Pulitzer Prize, and with it a place in literary history.

Like so many writers, he had to earn his laurels. The first agent who read his manuscript reckoned 'nobody was interested in that Irish stuff'; the second agent endorsed that opinion, though after reading the book, she showed it to an editor at Scribner. Within days Frank McCourt had a contract, went on to become an internationally known household name and, as the saying goes, the rest is history.

8

agents and publishers

'Jaw-jaw is better than war-war.' Harold MacMillan

'Publication is the Auction of the Mind of the Man.'
Emily Dickinson

8

agents and publishers

'Jaw-jaw is better than war-war.' Harold MacMillan

'Publication is the Auction of the Mind of the Man.'
Emily Dickinson

THE ROLE OF AN AGENT

The role of agents is to represent the author to the best of their ability and to the writer's greatest advantage. A good agent knows the marketplace, will promote a writer's work where it counts, demystifies contracts, is instrumental in selling on rights, and removes the burden of the administrative end of the 'business' of writing. In some cases an agent will provide editorial advice, creative support and long-term career planning, as well as marketing and promotion.

But one thing is for sure – an agent will only take on a writer whose work they are certain of selling, as their income is derived from commissions.

Finding an agent is not just a 'hey presto' matter of clicking your fingers. It's as difficult – some people say even more difficult – to get an agent as it is to get a publisher.

If you're aiming to be published by an Irish publisher, the need for an agent isn't as great as if you're looking for a British publisher. Irish publishers are approachable without an agent, and there are so few agents in Ireland that you only need the fingers of one hand to count them. Without contacts, it's difficult to get a UK publisher to even look at your work unless it comes through an agent. Indeed, in recent years, several of the commercial magazines aimed at the women's market have gone as far as only accepting short stories through an agent.

Literary agents, as they're known, are primarily a British phenomenon and there's a vast number to chose from. Agents play little part in the European publishing market, though they are an integral part of the American publishing scene.

Frequently, agents will have worked in publishing before setting up on their own or joining an existing literary agency. Publishing experience can be a plus as long as their expertise is relevant to placing work and beneficial in getting their authors the best deals.

Anyone can set themselves up as an agent. There are good and bad agents. So how can the newcomer differentiate in advance of signing up with an agent? Ideally, look for personal recommendation and word of mouth, though working on the premise that an agent taking on a new writer reduces the time given to them, some established authors can be reluctant to pass on the name of their agent. Agents can be adamant about not taking on new writers, though it has to be said that a good, promising writer who has an obvious future in the publishing world will find an agent, and may even have several to choose from.

I'm presuming that if you don't go for one of the Irish agents, listed further on, you'll look to the UK. A reasonable precaution in the British market is to narrow your choice to agents who are full members of the Association of Authors' Agents, founded in 1974. This association maintains a code of professional practice to which all members commit themselves.

Do you need an agent? Only you can answer that, but you'd be better off looking for an agent if you aren't familiar with:

- The publishing market and how it works.
- The right publishers to approach for your book and why.
- How to negotiate the best publishing deal, taking into account the current market climate.
- Understanding and being able to negotiate a contract.
- Making deals and selling yourself and your work.
- Lastly, consider the question that frequently drives authors to look for an agent: do you want to spend time that could be devoted to writing to handling the business end of your career?

So you've decided to look for an agent. Should you make your pitch to just the one and hope for the best, or should you make an application to several agents at the same time? There's nothing written in stone against making multiple submissions, though most agents would prefer you didn't, as after assessing and deciding to take on an author, they can discover the writer is on the point of signing with another agency.

Several top London agencies will not consider your application if you've placed your work with another agent. A point to bear in mind is that it can take agents several months to give you the yea or nay, so from a practical point of view where a writer is concerned, multiple submissions make sense.

The professional way to avoid bad feeling is to advise the agency along the lines of being happy to let it have sole sight of your manuscript for a certain period of time, say six weeks or two months. If you haven't heard back from them within your specified time, do give them a ring before sending your material out to another agency.

The next step is how to make that submission so that you'll convince the agent of your choice to take you on. This takes us back to professionalism. Think of the exercise as you would a job application for which you would be thoroughly prepared. You'll only get one chance to make your pitch. Take care that you don't sell yourself and your product short; take equal care that you don't make unrealistic assertions.

- Be professional in your approach.
- Make sure you've chosen the right agent for your book.
- Phone to check the format of your submission. Some agents want a complete work, others the opening chapters and more look for a synopsis and profiles of main characters as well as opening chapters. Some favour e-mail submissions and others look for hard copy.
- If hard copy, submit requirements typed in double spacing, on one side of A4 white paper.
- The covering letter should be short. Include reason/s why you wrote this specific book, the intended readership and other relevant information, such as if you're uniquely experienced to write your particular book.
- Any CVs should be short – one page is plenty. Keep it relevant and to the point.

Before taking you on as a client, the agent will usually ask to meet you. When English agents make the journey to Ireland, you can be sure they are interested. Treat this meeting as you would a job interview. This is business, not coffee or a lunch date with your new best friend. Be prepared to talk about yourself and your work.

A good agent knows the importance of a forthright character and a lively, outgoing personality for publicity purposes, and they will be checking your interpersonal skills. Don't be shy about asking questions.

Usually you'll be able to find out a little in advance about individual agents and agencies. *The Writers' & Artist's Yearbook* and *The Writers' Handbook* are reliable sources. Another outlet is www.author-network.com/agents.html, an Amazon-run site with a worldwide list of agents, though these are listed without order of preference.

The questions you need answered during your meeting are:
- What writers does the agent represent?
- Will the person you're meeting be handling your work? If not, may you meet whoever will represent you?
- What support does the agent offer?
- What percentage of books does the agent sell into the foreign markets? What countries?
- Does the agent have a representative in the US?

What if the agent you've prepared for so assiduously turns you down? Accept it. Whatever you do, don't pester him or her with a list of whys; don't ask for advice or editorial input. If agents provide editorial advice, it's only for their own clients. Chin up and move on to the next agent on your list – and you should have a list. If you get turned down a few times, perhaps you should review the standard of your work. You may need to return to your book to give it a thorough and impassioned overhaul.

There are many books written on various aspects of writing, and many courses available which are taught by published writers. I believe that anyone who attends a course wanting to be published should make sure that the course convener is a published writer themselves. There's a huge difference between teaching the theory of writing, and writing that's of publishable standard.

There's further information on courses in the section titled Professional Courses in Chapter 13. Perhaps you should go that route. Like any other skill, writing requires practice and practice is better with a knowledgeable, informed coach who has, as the saying goes, been there and done that.

LITERARY AGENTS IN IRELAND

The Book Bureau Literary Agency, 7 Duncairn Avenue, Bray, Co. Wicklow. Contact: Geraldine Nichol. Tel: 01 276 4996; fax: 01 276 4834; e-mail: the bookbureau@oceanfree.net. Full-length manuscripts (commission: home 10 per cent, USA/translation 20 per cent). Fiction preferred – thrillers, Irish novels, literary fiction, women's novels and general commercial. Preliminary letter, synopsis and three sample chapters. Return postage essential. Works with overseas agents.

Font International, 45 Victoria Road, Clontarf, Dublin 3. Tel: 01 853 2356; e-mail: info@fontwriters.com; website: www.fontwriters.com. Contact: Ita O'Driscoll. Adult fiction and non-fiction. See website for submission guidelines.

Marianne Gunne O'Connor, Morrison Chambers, Suite 17, 32 Nassau Street, Dublin 2. Contact: Marianne Gunne O'Connor. Tel: 01 677 9100; fax: 01 677 9101; e-mail: mgoclitagency@eircom.net. Founded 1996. Handles commercial and literary fiction, non-fiction, biography, health and children's fiction. Clients include Patrick McCabe, Morag Prunty, Claire Kilroy, Julie Dam, Cecelia Ahern, Paddy McMahon, Chris Binchy, Anita Notaro, Mike McCormack, Noelle Harrison, Claudia Carroll, Ken Bruen, John Lynch. No unsolicited manuscripts. Send preliminary enquiry letter plus half-page synopsis per e-mail. Commission: UK 15 per cent; overseas 20 per cent; film and TV 20 per cent. Translation rights handled by Vicki Satlow Literary Agency, Milan.

The Lisa Richards Agency, 46 Upper Baggot Street, Dublin 4. Contact: Faith O'Grady. Tel: 01 660 3534; fax: 01 660 3545; e-mail: faith@lisarichards.ie. Founded 1998. Fiction, non-fiction, children's. Commission: home 10 per cent, UK 15 per cent, USA/translation 20 per cent, film/TV 15 per cent. Approach with proposal and sample chapter for non-fiction, and three to four sample chapters and synopsis for fiction (SAE essential). Translation rights handled by the Marsh Agency Ltd in London. No reading fee.

Jonathan Williams Literary Agency, Rosney Mews, Upper Glenageary Road, Glenageary, Co. Dublin. Contact: Jonathan Williams. Tel: 01 280 3482; fax: 01 280 3482 Founded 1981. General fiction and non-fiction, preferably by Irish authors. Commission: home 10 per cent. Will suggest revisions; usually no reading fee unless a fast decision is required. Return postage appreciated. Sub-agents in Holland, Italy, France, Spain, Japan.

GETTING PUBLISHED

The Approach

The following section assumes you'll look for an Irish publisher, which, as noted previously, is easier for a new writer than trying for one in the UK, unless you have an agent. The majority of Irish publishers are eminently approachable and on the constant look-out for new voices. So how should you go about finding a publisher?

Initially, the best way to get a feel for the publishing market is to browse through the bookshops. Watch out for publishers who are publishing your style of book. Look them up on the internet, or ring and ask to be sent their list. Publishers' lists are catalogues with brief notes on the latest books they're bringing out as well as their past publications.

For instance, O'Brien Press in Rathgar, Dublin 6 is one of the most appropriate publishing houses to approach if you have a children's book, though it also has a comprehensive list of non-fiction. Poolbeg has a nose for discovering talented new women writers and has set international bestsellers Patricia Scanlan, Marian Keyes, Sheila O'Flanagan and Cathy Kelly on the road to success.

Lilliput Press goes for the more off-centre literary end of the market with recent titles such as *Larks' Eggs*, new and selected stories by Desmond Hogan; *The Atlantean Irish: Ireland's Oriental and Maritime Heritage* by Bob Quinn, the film-maker/writer; and *Wordgloss, A Cultural Lexicon* by Jim O'Donnell, adviser to the Taoiseach on the new Constitution. New Island favours non-fiction and high-quality fiction, such as Brian Lynch's acclaimed *The Winner of Sorrow*.

Blackstaff Press in Belfast specialises in adult fiction, as well as history and biography with titles such as *Dancers Dancing* by Éilis Ní Dhuibhne, shortlisted for the Orange prize; *Jenny Bristow Light* by Jenny Bristow and *A History of Ulster* by Jonathon Bardon, which has been updated and reprinted a number of times since its first publication.

After doing your market research, you'll hopefully be able to list several publishers who might be interested in your manuscript. Give them a ring. Get the name of the editor and ask to speak to him or her. Have the genre of your book, e.g. contemporary women's fiction, thriller, crime, saga, the period and where it's set and anything else salient at your fingertips.

A consolatory word here about identifying genre, which can be rather off-putting for the beginner. J.K. Rowling has said she was unaware until after it was published that *Harry Potter and the Philosopher's Stone* was a fantasy novel. She has never finished reading *The Lord of the Rings* and hasn't even read all of C.S. Lewis's Narnia novels, to which her books are often compared.

Remember, you're starting the process of selling both your book and yourself. While publishing houses don't turn down manuscripts because their authors aren't vocal or good with the media, a writer who is and who is passionate about their book has an edge and is a more attractive prospect.

If the editor expresses an interest in reading your manuscript, some will ask for the whole manuscript (details about presentation are given below), while others want only the first three chapters (send the opening chapters). Still others look for plot outline, character details and synopsis. Usually at this stage editors favour hard copy, i.e. printout pages, rather than e-mail, discs or CDs.

Presentation of Manuscript

Listed below are the general requirements for presenting your manuscript:

- White A-4 paper.
- Double spaced with generous margins on the top, bottom and sides, about 3.5 to 4 mm.
- Times New Roman, 12 point font is a universally acceptable typeface because of readability.
- Start each chapter on a new page.

- Number pages consecutively throughout.
- The front page should contain the title of the book and your name in 16 point font, bold and centred; your address; your contact numbers in the bottom right-hand corner; and the number of words, date and the copyright sign, followed by your initials, in the left-hand corner.
- Put everything into a padded envelope, with return postage (which you hope won't be required), post it and wait.

Before sending out your manuscript, it's advisable to check publishers' specific requirements. Poolbeg Press, publishers of commercial fiction, currently favouring issue-led books, receives in the region of 2,500 unsolicited manuscripts per year, of which about twenty are published. Guidelines for submission to Poolbeg include the following:

- Manuscripts are submitted at the author's own risk. Do not send original, a copy will do.
- Check spelling and punctuation.
- Initially, send a synopsis plus first six chapters, with CV and short biography of yourself.
- Full manuscripts should be bound in a plastic spiral binding for easy reading.
- Manuscripts should be addressed to Paula Campbell, Publisher, Poolbeg Press, 123 Grange Hill, Baldoyle, Dublin 13. It normally takes six to eight weeks to get back to the author.

Because publishers receive so many submissions, there's frequently a delay in responding, especially to new and unknown writers, and it's not usual for publishers to acknowledge receipt of manuscripts. If you haven't heard back after six weeks, give them a ring and ask when you can hope for a decision. After that, there's nothing you can do but wait and hope.

As with agents, there are two schools of thought about multiple submissions to publishers. While publishers may frown on the idea, until a writer has found a home with a publishing house, submitting your manuscript to several publishers simultaneously does speed up the process.

You can wait over three months for a decision from a publisher, and if you are turned down, you have to start the whole process again and perhaps wait another three months for a decision. Posting off half a dozen copies to selected publishers is more professional and efficient, and considerably cuts down on the limbo time of waiting, as well as offering a modicum of hope when one manuscript is returned.

If you've only sent the opening chapters, it's a good sign if the publisher calls for the remainder, though don't start celebrating yet. That old saying of there being 'many a slip 'twixt cup and lip' is eminently applicable to publishing.

Presuming your manuscript is taken up by one of the publishing houses, you'll usually be invited in to meet the publisher, editor and perhaps the marketing person, which is good because every book, no matter how wonderful the contents are, needs a marketing package. They'll be assessing you, your appearance and potential for media interviews, and sussing out if you've another book in you. Understandably, publishers are reluctant to invest in a one-book author. Give them what they want – dress in your best and be at your most scintillating. This is the PR game. Play it in public and know it's not real, and afterwards gratefully close your hall door and revert to being couch potato or video exercising dervish.

A question that's frequently asked is whether you have to tell the publishers that you've made multiple submissions. You don't. At this stage it's not their business, but if asked, don't lie. Once you have a signed contract, be sure to drop a line to the other publishers, thanking them for their time and consideration and explaining that you have an offer for the publication of your book.

THE CONTRACT

We're still presuming you haven't got an agent. But now that you've got a publisher, an Irish agent may take you on. An agent will save you from negotiating the minefield of a contract, and may even sell you on the foreign market, for which he or she will take between 10 to 20 per cent of your earnings from your book.

Courtesy of the Irish Writers' Union, you can download a sample contract from its website, www.ireland-writers.com. The majority of publishing contracts look long and complicated, and they are. *Caveat scriptor* – author beware. Don't believe a publisher who tells you they have standard contracts which are non-negotiable. There is always room for negotiation, though the first-time author doesn't have much clout.

As authors, you're advised to keep copies of all correspondence, save e-mails, make notes of what was said during telephone calls and confirm it in writing.

The main points to be aware of in your contract are as follows:

Agreement

In the publishing world, 'agreement' means 'contract'. Once signed, a contract is legally binding on both parties, i.e. author and publisher. No contract should be entered into lightly, no matter how eager you are to have your work published. What you give away in terms of rights, you may never be able to take back.

Copyright

Copyright means actual ownership of the intellectual property. Copyright is vested in the author of a written work or the creator of a photograph or picture. A publisher does not buy the copyright when a contract is negotiated, he merely

licenses the right to publish the work. Authors are advised never to sell their copyright. They are further advised to send a copy of the completed manuscript with their name, address and date on the first page by registered post addressed to themselves. Request that the post office stamp across the seal, and do not open the package when it arrives. Keep it in a secure place or give it to your solicitor. This establishes beyond question the date of completion of the work – and could be important should anyone question your authorship at some future date.

Duration and Scope

Authors are advised against granting indefinite rights. Periods of ten, fifteen or twenty years are most common, though if the publisher isn't reprinting, you do hear of rights being returned to the author three or four years after first publication.

Editing

Editing can be the most difficult aspect of the author/publisher relationship. An author is perfectly at liberty to reject editorial suggestions. Remember, you own the work. However, also remember that it's in the publisher's best interest to ensure that the work is as successful as possible. A good editor can substantially improve a work.

Advance

Publishers, especially smaller publishers, sometimes claim they don't pay advances. As with every other aspect of the contract, this too is negotiable. The size of any advance is based on the initial print run and projected sales. It's not reasonable to expect a publisher to pay a larger advance than he feels the book will earn back. With this understanding, however, authors are advised to negotiate for the largest possible advance. Money paid to you further down the line will probably be diminished by inflation. A sizeable advance encourages the publisher to promote your book.

Schedule of Royalties

The more established and successful a writer, the better position he or she is in to negotiate royalties. First-time authors typically start at the bottom of the scale, but even so they should be mindful of the possibilities of negotiation upward as their careers progress. Perhaps we should aim to achieve J.K. Rowling's reputed £2 for each book sold.

Ideally, the royalties should be based on the list price (gross price of the book) and not net receipts. The list price is the price on the back of the book, i.e. the published price; net receipts is the money the publisher receives after the booksellers' discount (usually 33.33 per cent but often rising to 60 per cent) has been deducted.

Subsidiary Rights

Depending on the type of book, subsidiary rights may be extremely valuable, as in the case of a work subsequently made into a movie. If a book has this potential, the author may wish to retain such rights for themselves, or ask for a larger advance if the publisher wants those rights. Authors should aim to offer the publisher only those rights which the author believes the publisher can properly exploit. Subsidiary rights can be independently negotiated. Therefore, in the contract such rights should be differentiated, and not lumped together in one catch-all clause.

Reports and Payments

From the author's point of view, it's preferable for the publisher to calculate and pay royalties twice a year. This is commonplace practice abroad. Bi-annual accounting cuts down the delay between payments to the author. If payments are made yearly, then monies earned on a title in January won't be paid until at least March of the following year, during which time the interest on the money keeps mounting up and accruing in the publisher's pocket and isn't passed on to the author.

Writers are advised to keep detailed records of all monies due and received, and the dates on which payments are due.

Reversion of Rights

An out-of-print title earns no money for the author. If the title goes out of print, send a written request to the publisher asking that they either reprint within the period specified in the contract or revert rights to you. It's possible to resell out-of-print titles to another publisher.

Termination of Contract

This can be the most important clause in a contract. There are many reasons why an author may wish to terminate a contract. Once a contract is signed, however, and therefore legally binding, it may only be terminated by mutual agreement or if one side can prove the contract has been breached. It's much easier to get into trouble than get out of it, so be sure before you sign.

Unacceptable Clauses

Experienced authors rely on their agents here, who routinely delete unacceptable clauses from offered contracts. The first contract a publisher offers a beginning writer is likely to be one-sided on the publisher's behalf. Don't simply sign it, thinking you'll never be offered another.

Option

Many publishing contracts contain some form of option clauses. This gives the publisher the privilege of publishing the author's next book or books – if he wishes. But be advised – this does not assure the author another sale! It merely means that the next book will be tied up for a period when it might well be sold more profitably elsewhere. Option clauses are one-sided agreements binding authors but not publishers and, if wished by the author, should be struck out.

Overpayment

A reference to overpayment in a contract is another way of getting the author to agree to joint accounting – the deduction of sums owing under other contracts. Therefore, a writer who writes more than one book with a publisher may find that his advance for the second book is charged back to the royalties of the first one, so in effect he may never receive any royalties.

Each publishing contract and book should be treated as a separate venture. You're advised not to accept any clause that allows for joint accounting under any name, or allows the publisher to deduct sums owed by the author under another contract. Remember, the publisher is a businessperson who has agreed to publish the book at their risk and expense. If a book doesn't make money, it was the risk the publisher contractually agreed to take. The author shouldn't have to pay for it out of other books.

In a nutshell, signing a contract means:

- You agree to deliver your book to the publishers – usually on disk, CD or by e-mail as well as hard copy – on or before an agreed date, with contents as discussed.
- If necessary, you have to get copyright clearance, organise photos, maps or diagrams and, if required, bear the cost.
- You guaranteed there's nothing libellous in your book, and contract to indemnify your publishers if libel actions arise.
- If an index is required, then in most cases you have to supply it at your own expense, though this can be negotiable.

- Time permitting, you get to look at the cover. In theory the author has no say in design, binding, jacket blurb, quality of paper, printing or advertising. In practice, there's usually a mutually beneficial co-operation between publisher and author.
- It's up to you to read, check, correct and sign the proof within the time specified by the publisher.
- You're expected to promote your book by being available for newspaper, magazine, radio and television interviews and appearances.

ELECTRONIC PUBLISHING

Book publishing is in the middle of a revolution, with more changes happening now than in all the years since Gutenberg and his printing press put those monks and scribes with their quill pens out of work. Advances in technology have brought different options to the publishing market, though the traditional method is still the preferred and more credible route.

Google throws up in excess of 171 million e-publishing sites on a preliminary search, so if you decide to go the electronic publishing route, choice of publisher will not be one of your problems! Though 'swizz' is the word that frequently comes to mind when charting electronic publishing.

All the major publishing houses have websites they promote their books on. This isn't the same as the companies that offer to promote or publish work electronically. E-publishers range from those who post sample chapters and then charge readers a fee for the complete work to professional e-book developers who format books to fit on your computer screen, Blackberry or iPod. The text can be either printed out or read on screen.

In many ways, print and electronic publishing are not dissimilar. An author still has to write, edit and submit his books. The book is either accepted or rejected. Don't be fooled – e-publishing isn't an easy route. The majority of e-publishers are so inundated with manuscripts that they regularly have to close submissions. They can afford to be as selective as print publishers, and currently more than 90 per cent of submissions are rejected. Many e-publishers double as online book-sellers.

You can access a directory of e-publishers, their submission requirements and general guidelines at www.ebookcrossroads.com.

SELF–PUBLISHING

The Irish self-publishing success story has to be Roddy Doyle's *The Commitments*, his first novel published in 1987 to critical acclaim. This story of a working-class Irish band put together by young Jimmy Rabbitte 'committed to bringing soul to Ireland' was adapted into a movie in 1991.

Let's not forget Mary Kenny, who in 2004 self-published *Allegiance*, a play about the relationship between Winston Churchill and Michael Collins under the imprint Kildare Street Books.

Then there's G.P. Taylor, the Anglican rector who self-published his debut novel *Shadowmancer* in 2002. Within weeks he was signed to Faber & Faber and acquired an American publisher. *Shadowmancer* became an international bestseller, was translated into 42 languages and is to be turned into a film and video game.

Self-publishing is an increasingly acceptable way to be published. There is seemingly unlimited information on the internet about self-publishing, with a choice of more than two million sites. True self-publishing gives authors considerable control over the production and distribution of their books. In a self-published book, the name decided by the author as his or her publishing house must appear on the copyright page of the book. In addition, the ISBN number must be registered by the ISBN Agency to that author as publisher.

A self-published book is the property of the author. If an author chooses to employ a distributor, this can be shown in the 'Distributor (if different from Publisher)' portion of the form sent to the ISBN Agency prior to publication.

VANITY PUBLISHING

The Advertising Standards Authority's definition of vanity publishing, 1997, reads, 'Vanity publishing, also self-styled (often inaccurately) as "subsidy", "joint-venture", "shared-responsibility" or even "self" publishing, is a service whereby authors are charged to have their work published. Vanity publishers generally offer to publish a book for a specific fee, or offer to include short stories, poems or other literary or artistic material in an anthology, which the authors are then invited to buy.'

The general consensus from reputable sources within the industry on vanity publishing is: don't.

The difference between vanity and mainstream publishers is that the latter invests in the promotion of a book and makes their profit from the sale of copies of the book, whereas vanity publishers make their money from up-front charges.

One of the main disadvantages of being published by a vanity publisher is lack of credibility within the industry. Vanity published books are seen as badly produced, over-priced, poorly jacketed and lacking marketing support.

The majority of booksellers and library suppliers are unwilling to handle vanity published books and it's difficult to get credible, book-enhancing publicity. Reviewers are reluctant to review them, and unless the author is a 'character' in his or her own right, the print media, radio and TV are even more reluctant to give them interview time.

Anyone who is either looking for a vanity publisher or who has experienced problems with one should look into Johnathon Clifford's website at www.vanitypublishing.info. His free advice pack on the subject of vanity publishing will answer all your questions.

agents and publishers

BOOK PUBLISHERS

Listed below, in alphabetical order, are some of the main book publishers in Ireland, the majority of which are members of The Irish Book Publishers' Association (CLÉ), a cross-border organisation founded in 1970 so that publishers could share expertise and resources. Your best bet for a full list of Irish-based publishers is *The Writers' & Artists' Yearbook* or *The Writers' Handbook.*

Before approaching any publishing house, it's advisable to study its list of current and back issue books, which can be accessed via its website.

Appletree Press Ltd, 14 Howard Street South, Belfast, BT7 IAP. Tel: 028 9024 3074; fax: 028 9024 6756; e-mail: reception@appletree.ie; website: www.appletree.ie. Director: John Murphy. Founded 1974. Specialising in gift books, biography, cookery, guidebooks, history, Irish interest, literary criticism, music, photography, social studies, sport, travel.

Blackstaff Press Ltd, 4c Heron Wharf, Sydenham Business Park, Belfast BT3 9LE. Tel: 028 9045 5006; fax: 028 9046 6237; e-mail: info@blackstaffpress.com; website: www.blackstaffpress.com. Managing editor: Patsy Horton. Founded 1971. Specialising in adult fiction, poetry, biography, history, sport, politics, cookery, natural history, humour.

Brandon/Mount Eagle Publications, Cooleen, Dingle, Co. Kerry. Tel: 066 915 1463; fax: 066 915 1234; website: www.brandonbooks.com. Publisher: Steve MacDonogh. Founded 1982. Specialising in fiction, biography, current affairs. No unsolicited mss.

Cló Iar-Chonnachta Teo, Indreabhán, Conamara, Co. Galway. Tel: 091 593307; fax: 091 593362; e-mail: cic@iol.ie; website: www.cic.ie. Director: Micheál Ó Conghaile; general manager: Deirdre O'Toole. Founded 1985. Specialising in

Irish-language novels, short stories, plays, poetry, songs, history and cassettes (writers reading from their works in Irish and English). Promotes translation of contemporary Irish fiction and poetry into other languages.

The Columba Press, 55a Spruce Avenue, Stillorgan Industrial Park, Blackrock, Co. Dublin. Tel: 01 294 2556; fax: 01 294 2564; e-mail: info@columba.ie; website: www.columba.ie. Publisher and managing director: Seán O'Boyle. Founded 1985. Specialising in religion, including pastoral handbooks, spirituality, theology, liturgy and prayer, counselling and self-help.

Imprint: **Currach Press** specialises in general non-fiction.

Cork University Press, Youngline Industrial Estate, Pouladuff Road, Togher, Cork. Tel: 021 490 2980; fax: 021 431 5329; e-mail: corkunip@ucc.ie; website: www.corkuniversitypress.com. Publisher: Mike Collins. Founded 1925. Specialising in Irish literature, history, cultural studies, medieval studies, English literature, musicology, poetry, translations.

Imprints: **Attic Press** and **Atrium** specialise in books by and about women in the areas of social and political comment, women's studies, reference guides and handbooks.

The Educational Company of Ireland, Ballymount Road, Walkinstown, Dublin 12. Tel: 01 450 0611; fax: 01 450 0993; e-mail: info@edco.ie; website: www.edco.ie. Publisher: Frank Fahy. Founded 1910. Educational manuscripts on all subjects in English or Irish language.

CJ Fallon, Ground Floor, Block B, Liffey Valley Office Campus, Dublin 22. Tel: 01 616 6400; fax: 01 616 6499; e-mail: editorial@cjfallon.ie; Editor: N White. Educational textbooks. Founded 1927.

Flyleaf Press, 4 Spencer Villas, Glenageary, Co. Dublin. Tel: 01 284 5906; e-mail: flyleaf@indigo.ie; website: www.flyleaf.ie.

Managing editor: James Ryan. Irish family history. Founded 1988.

Folens Publishers, Hibernian Industrial Estate, Greenhills Road, Tallaght, Dublin 24. Tel: 01 413 7200; fax: 01 413 7282; website: www.folens.ie. Chairman: Dirk Folens. Educational (primary, secondary, comprehensive and technical) in English and Irish. Founded 1956.

Imprint: **Blackwater**: General non-fiction, Irish interest, children's fiction. Founded 1993.

Four Courts Press, 7 Malpas Street, Dublin 7. Tel: 01 453 4668; fax: 01 433 4672; e-mail: info@four-courts-press.ie; website: www.four-courts-press.ie. Managing director: Michael Adams. Founded 1970. Academic books in the humanities, especially history, Celtic and medieval studies, art, theology.

The Gallery Press, Loughcrew, Oldcastle, Co. Meath. Tel: 049 854 1779; fax: 049 854 1779; e-mail: gallery@indigo.ie; website: www.gallerypress.com. Founded 1970. Editor/publisher: Peter Fallon. Poetry, drama, occasionally fiction by Irish authors.

Gill & Macmillan Ltd, Hume Avenue, Park West, Dublin 12. Tel: 01 500 9500; fax: 01 500 9599; website: www.gillmacmillan.ie. Biography or memoirs, educational (secondary, university), history, literature, cookery, current affairs, guidebooks, popular fiction. Founded 1968. Commissioning editor for general titles: Fergal Tobin, ftobin@gillmacmillan.ie. Approach with synopsis and sample chapters.

Hodder Headline Ireland, 8 Castlecourt, Castleknock, Dublin 15. Tel: 01 824 6288; fax: 01 824 6289; e-mail: info@hhireland.ie; website: www.hhireland.ie. Publisher: Ciara Considine. General fiction, non-fiction, memoir/biography, sport, politics, current affairs, music. Submissions guidelines – Fiction: First three chapters and single page synopsis/blurb. Non-fiction: Proposal and chapter layout. No e-mail submissions. Enclose SAE.

Irish Academic Press Ltd, 44 Northumberland Road, Ballsbridge, Dublin 4. Tel: 01 668 8244; fax: 01 660 1610; e-mail: info@iap.ie; website: www.iap.ie. Directors: Stewart Cass, Frank Cass. Administrator: Rachel Milotte. Scholarly books, especially 19th- and 20th-century history, literature, heritage and culture. Founded 1974.

Imprints: **Irish University Press, Irish Academic Press**.

The Liffey Press, Ashbrook House, 10 Main Street, Raheny, Dublin 5. Tel: 01 851 1458; fax: 01 851 1459; e-mail: info@theliffeypress.com; website: ww.theliffeypress.com. Publisher and managing director: David Givens, dgivens@theliffeypress.com; Editor: Brian Langan, blangan@theliffeypress.com. Non-fiction books of Irish interest.

The Lilliput Press Ltd, 62-63 Sitric Road, Dublin 7. Tel: 01 671 1647; fax: 01 671 1233; e-mail: info@lilliputpress.ie; website: www.lilliputpress.ie. Managing director: Antony Farrell. General and Irish literature, essays, memoir, biography/autobiography, fiction, criticism; Irish history; philosophy; Joyce and contemporary culture; nature and environment. Founded 1974.

Mentor Books, 43 Furze Road, Sandyford Industrial Estate, Dublin 18. Tel: 01 295 2112; fax: 01 295 2114; e-mail: mentorbooks.ie; website: www.mentorbooks.ie. Managing director: Daniel McCarthy; managing editor: Claire Haugh. General: fiction, non-fiction, children's guidebooks, biographies, history. Education (secondary): languages, history, geography, business, maths, science. No unsolicited mss. Founded 1980.

Mercier Press, Douglas Village, Cork. Tel: 021 489 9858; fax: 021 489 9887; e-mail: books@mercierpress.ie; website:

www.mercierpress.ie. Directors: J.F. Spillane, M.P. Feehan. Irish literature, folklore, history, politics, humour, academic, current affairs, health, mind and spirit, general non-fiction, children's. Founded 1944.

Imprint: **Marino Books**.

Morrigan Book Company, Killala, Co. Mayo. Tel: 096 32555; e-mail: morriganbooks@online.ie. Publisher: Gerry Kennedy. Non-fiction only: general Irish interest, biography, history, folklore and mythology. Approach by preliminary letter. Founded 1979.

New Island, 2 Brookside, Dundrum Road, Dundrum, Dublin 14. Tel: 01 298 6867/298 9937; fax: 01 298 2783; website: www.newisland.ie. Directors: Edwin Higel (managing), Fergal Stanley. Literary fiction, popular fiction, current affairs, biography, memoir, poetry, drama, humour, sport. Founded 1992. Editorial manager: Deirdre Nolan, editor@newisland.ie. Submit two chapters and a synopsis, and enclose SAE.

The O'Brien Press Ltd, 20 Victoria Road, Rathgar. Dublin 6. Tel: 01 492 3333; e-mail: books@obrien.ie; website: www.obrien.ie. Directors: Michael O'Brien, Ide Ní Laoghaire, Ivan O'Brien. Founded 1974. Adult: biography, local history, true crime, sport, humour, reference. Requirements: Children's fiction for all ages. Solos (3+), Pandas (5), Flyers (6+), Red Flag (8+), substantial novels (10+) – contemporary, historical, fantasy. Unsolicited mss (sample chapters only) synopses and ideas for books welcome.

On Stream Publications Ltd, Currabaha, Cloughroe, Blarney, Co. Cork. Tel: 021 438 5798; e-mail: info@onstream.ie; website www.onstream.ie. Publisher: Rosalind Crowley. Non-fiction: cookery, wine, travel, local history, academic and practical books. Founded 1986.

Penguin Ireland, 25 St Stephen's Green, Dublin 2. Tel: 01 661 7695; fax: 01 661 7696; e-mail: info@penguin.ie; website: www.penguin.ie. Managing director: Michael McLoughlin, senior editor: Patricia Deevy, editor: Brendan Barrington. Commercial and literary fiction and non-fiction. See website for submission guidelines. Founded 2002.

Pillar Press, Ladywell, Thomastown, Co. Kilkenny. Tel: 056 772 4901; e-mail: info@pillarpress.ie; website www.pillarpress.ie. Directors and editors: Stephen Buck/Marian O'Neill. Literary fiction, poetry and short stories. Submissions in form of one-page synopsis plus 30 pages (maximum) sample. No e-mail submissions. SAE for return. Founded 2005.

Poolbeg Press Ltd, 123 Grange Hill, Baldoyle, Dublin 13. Tel: 01 832 1477; fax: 01 832 1430; e-mail: poolbeg@poolbeg.com; website: www.poolbeg.com. Directors: Kieran Devlin (managing), Paula Campbell (publisher). Popular fiction, non-fiction, current affairs. See website for submission guidelines. Founded 1976.

TownHouse, Trinity House, Charleston Road, Ranelagh, Dublin 6. Tel: 01 497 2399; fax: 01 497 0927; e-mail: books@townhouse.ie; website: www.townhouse.ie. Directors: Treasa Coady, Jim Coady. General illustrated non-fiction: art, archaeology and biography. Founded 1981.

Imprints: **TownHouse, Simon and Schuster/TownHouse, Pocket/TownHouse, Scribner/TownHouse**.

University College Dublin Press, Newman House, 86 St Stephen's Green, Dublin 2. Tel: 01 716 7397; fax: 01 716 7211; e-mail: ucdpress@ucd.ie; website: www.ucdpress.ie. Executive editor: Barbara Mennell. Founded 1995. Purely academic. Irish studies, history and politics, literary studies.

9

research

'To write it, it took three months; to conceive it – three minutes; to collect the data in it – all my life.' F. Scott Fitzgerald

THE ART OF RESEARCH

Research, whether major or minor, is a vital part of writing. There is nothing mysterious about research, it simply involves knowing what you require and where to source it. A good starting point can be the Google search engine on the World Wide Web. It's particularly important in journalism to be able to source relevant material, and if you're lucky, on special occasions, like Mary Kenny, you'll get a 'happenstance' revelation when your research takes you into the realms of an unexpected interview route:

> A piece of research I did in south-east England, interviewing 25 young women who had been pregnant before the age of 15 was an absolute eye-opener into another world. They had all been given very specific sex education (bar one, probably): some were taught, at the age of 11, how to put on a condom, with the teacher using a banana as a classroom model. This made no practical impact whatsoever. To these kids, having early sex and getting pregnant was simply 'doing what comes naturally' and no amount of contraception would have stopped them. Some were sweet youngsters, doing their best, but so far from the middle-class model of how human beings might behave, given 'choices' and 'information', that they might as well be on the planet Neptune. A common thread in their experiences, though, was that most lacked a continuous, protective or loving father.

While research plays a major role in most non-fiction, it should not be allowed to dominate or to intrude in fiction. Research is part of the back story – and the key word here is 'back'.

When you move away from the comfortable boundaries of writing about what you know, research becomes inevitable, and can add a lot to your story. A chase throughout part of a city needs detailed knowledge of that city; if you're cooking an Irish stew, knowing the ingredients adds a delicious note of authenticity; when you locate a scene in an art gallery, the background paintings, sculptures and ambience enhance your characters' actions.

However, where research is concerned, be wary of ending up with the tail wagging the dog. You're not writing a research paper.

DIRECTORIES and THE WEB

Directories

There are all kinds of directories covering a variety of subjects, including:

- Golden Pages and Yellow Pages. Look at the index at the back under your topic. It's amazing what information an unsolicited phone call can bring.
- Independent Directory for street maps, bus timetables, restaurants, holidays (www.independentdirectory.ie).

The Web

The web is an increasingly invaluable source of research. Simply by accessing Google, keying in a few descriptive words or a short phrase and hitting the Enter key, you can throw up a mine of information on your subject, but be aware that many sites are not necessarily accurate or up-to-date.

For efficient research from websites, select your key words with care and make them as specific as possible.

LIBRARIES

Libraries are a joy to work in and invariably the staff are helpful beyond belief. Public libraries in Northern Ireland are divided into regions:
- Belfast Education and Library Board.
- North Eastern Education and Library Board.
- Southern Education and Library Board.
- South Eastern Education and Library Board.
- Western Education and Library Board.

All can be accessed via www.ni-libraries.net. As well as the usual informational links, these libraries offer details on Lifelong Learning and eGovernment.

Listed below, in alphabetical order, are some of the libraries in the Republic of Ireland.

Central Catholic Library, 74 Merrion Square, Dublin 2. Tel: 01 676 1264; website: www.catholiclibrary.ie. Specialises in philosophy, religion and social history. If you ring in advance specifying your requirements, preliminary ground work will be carried out for you. To become a member requires a standard application form, plus a guarantor.

The Chester Beatty Library, The Clock Tower Building, Dublin Castle, Dublin 2. Tel: 01 407 0750; website: www.cbl.ie The reference library includes manuscripts and scrolls of Chinese, Japanese, Burmese, biblical, Arabic, Tibetan and Mongolian origin. Apply for research facility to the director.

The Contemporary Music Centre Ltd, 19 Fishamble Street, Temple Bar, Dublin 8. Tel: 01 673 1922; website: www.cmc.ie. National archive and resource centre for new music, supporting the work of composers throughout the Republic and Northern Ireland.

Corporation and County Council Libraries are listed under 'Libraries' in the relevant Golden Pages. Of special interest to researchers are:

- Dublin City Libraries HQ, 138-144 Pearse Street, Dublin 2, which houses **Dublin City Library and Archive**. Tel: 01 674 4999; e-mail: dublinstudies@dublincity.ie; cityarchives@dublincity.ie.
- The Ilac Centre, Henry Street, Dublin, 1, which houses **The Central Library**, tel: 01 873 4333; **Children's Library**, tel: 01 873 4333; **Business Information Centre**, tel: 01 873 3996; **Music Library**, tel: 01 873 4333.

For further information, log on to www.dublincitypublic litraries.ie.

The Irish Architectural Archive, 73 Merrion Square, Dublin 2. Tel: 01 676 3430; website: www.iarc.ie. Anyone wishing to research architectural matters is welcome.

The Law Library, Four Courts, Dublin 7. Tel: 01 872 0622; website: www.lawlibrary.ie. Library is open only to members of the bar.

Mercer Library, The Royal College of Surgeons, St Stephen's Green, Dublin 2. Tel: 01 478 0200; website: www.rcsi.ie/library. Though not open to the general public, it can't be beaten for researching medical matters.

The National Library of Ireland, Kildare Street, Dublin 2. Tel: 01 603 0200; website: www.nli.ie. Offers the crème de la crème of research facilities for historical matters, though as seating is so limited, would-be researchers are encouraged to use their local library if material is available. Ring in for details on readers' tickets.

Universities have comprehensive libraries and research facilities, but you'll probably need a reading card, usually only available to those who have studied there. It's best to make an e-mail query.
- Belfast: The Queen's University (www.qub.ac.uk/library).
- Cork: University College Cork, UCC (www.ucc.ie/library).
- Derry: McGill University (www.iirc.mcgill.ca/library).

- Dublin: University College Dublin UCD (www.ucd.ie/library); Trinity College, TCD (www.tcd.ie/library).
- Galway: NUI Galway (www.nuigalway.ie/library).
- Limerick: University of Limerick (www.ul.ie/library).

RESEARCH MATERIAL

When you're researching, use a notebook, a laptop, an electronic notebook or make a photocopy, usually available for a small charge in the majority of research venues. A generally quoted statistic is that for every 1,000 words you're going to write on a subject you're not familiar with, you need in the region of 5,000 words of research.

Create files and cuttings. Well-maintained filing cabinets are an invaluable research tool. When you read documents, features and books, file notes from these too. But don't become overly reliant on cuttings – they go out of date and checking back is advisable.

Research is heady and exciting and it's all too easy to lose the run of ourselves. Be ruthless about keeping to your primary focus. Be careful you aren't lured down blind alleys of interesting information. Resist the urge to get carried away exploring the route of minor points and minor characters. For example, when researching the architecture and furnishings of the Victorian era for a fairly long feature on a socialite of the time, I got so carried away that I became a mine of information on the history of fitted carpets, exercise horses, plate warmers and boudoirs that I almost forgot my commission was a historical profile.

Or take the example of an enthusiastic student full of ideas, a good researcher and writer hoping to break into journalism. He interested a feature editor in running a piece on the Danish storyteller Hans Christian Andersen a week before the 130th anniversary of his death on August 4 2005. But the would-be journalist got so carried away with research and accumulated so much material that he was unable to marshal the relevant facts for the 800-word feature, and missed his chance.

At the outset of your writing career, concentrate on researching, writing and selling one piece at a time. But do make a note of any other feature ideas you stumble across during research that could be of use later on.

The material acquired from research invariably shapes a journalistic piece or non-fiction writing, though stubborn determination to use every scrap of information you have unearthed, relevant or not, can ruin a piece of writing. Early on in my writing career, a commissioning editor said, 'The sign of a true professional is being able to let go of your darlings.' She was right. What you leave out is as important as what you include. Research not immediately used won't be wasted. Keep it. Its value in the future will more than reward your restraint.

Returning to features for a moment, never be content with writing just one or two pieces about a topic when your research will keep you funded to sell different angles on your subject to different papers, trade and specialist magazines and overseas. The main hardship, as you'll discover, in wringing research dry is that you'll get tired of the subject; you'll be delighted to see the back of it and to move onto pastures new.

NOTEBOOK

A writer's notebook is a vital piece of equipment and should never leave your side. As noted previously, Mary Kenny is a notebook aficionado. Into it you can jot down facts, ideas, quotations, useful and useless bits of information, colourful phrases, snatches of thoughts, lines of dialogue, moods and emotions.

Your notebook comes into its own when inspiration becomes sluggish. You can use your imagination to start chain reactions between apparently unrelated ideas.

Be curious about human motives, human error, love and hatred. Develop a fascination with people – the way they look, the clothes they wear, the environment they create; watch body language and social interaction; discover the books they read and their mannerisms of talking. Listen to conversations, unashamedly eavesdrop.

Note down items of interest that you hear, sentences you read, snatches of dialogue that appeal to you and quotable quotes. Pieces like these combust off each other and, fuelled by the imagination, trigger ideas.

A page of your notebook could read something along the lines of the following:

- Women look great on boats and horses, but terrible in the bar afterwards.
- Description of house – a cavernous depot for the storage of marital silences.
- Call Money – money at call and at short notice.
- Double income dinner parties.
- Dancing – the vertical expression of horizontal desire.
- For all her thinness she had an almost breakfast cereal air of health, a soap and lemon cleanness.
- He bent his head at every step and seemed to be continually bowing.
- Window shopping – parading up and down a shopping street with intent to covet rather than to buy.

- 'If we end up together, this is the most romantic day of my life. If we don't I'm a slut.'
- Beautiful young people are accidents of nature. Beautiful old people create themselves.
- A sound of low fugitive laughter.

CONTACT BOOK

As mentioned in Chapter 1, Getting Started, from the beginning of your writing career it's beneficial to keep a contact book. It needn't be anything fancy, though a durable cover helps, as it should see a lot of wear.

Writers often need fast access to accurate professional information. A list of contacts, depending on your subjects and theme of your writing, could include a banker, bookie, solicitor, psychologist, psychiatrist, architect, stockbroker, a few socialites, fundraisers or perhaps an interior designer. If you cover crime, you'll need access to a garda or a PSNI contact.

Few freelance journalists write on general subjects – most develop a speciality subject and/or linked subjects. To do so professionally, it's necessary to build a contact book which contains sources' phone numbers, addresses, faxes, mobile numbers, e-mail addresses and websites. Make sure to back up details on a computer database.

You'll be attending meetings, press conferences and launches and talking to the spokespeople of pressure groups, political parties, companies, etc. looking for your next story, all of which eats into your time. But if you have a good panel of sources, you'll get ideas for stories, details of events, quotes and specialist information.

10

right
to
write

'Look in thy heart and write.' Sir Philip Sidney

WRITING FOR THERAPY

Anton Chekhov advised actors, 'If you want to work on your acting, work on yourself.' The same advice applies to writers. Using writing as a therapy has a double-edged benefit. It both improves our writing skills (remember that Chapter 1 opened by asking you to write about a situation that you were currently trying to metabolise), and secondly, it allows us to get to know our inner selves better. The majority of the finest writers are able to take a wry look at themselves and live with what they see.

Writing helps us to map our interior world. Part of laying the track is letting ourselves imagine in what direction we might like to lay it. This gives us a sense of emotional geography.

The therapy of writing is well documented. Writing from the heart forms an integral part of many counselling sessions, as does writing and destroying letters to those who have offended, hurt or perhaps affected our lives.

The first trick in therapeutic writing is to start where you are. It's a luxury to be in the mood to write. It's a blessing, but it's not a necessity. Writing is like breathing – it's possible to learn to do it well, but the point is to do it, no matter what.

The act of writing, the aiming of getting it right, is as thrilling and as exciting as drawing back a bow and hitting a creative bull's eye. Nothing beats scoring that phrase or sentence that precisely expresses what you see shimmering on the horizon of your mind. Those phrases or sentences alone are worth the chase, but the chase itself and the situations you catch out of the corner of your eye are worth recording too. It's great when you write well, but it's almost equally great when you write. Period.

Wherever you are right now is your entry point, the place for you to begin writing. You don't need to put out the cat, fill the car with petrol or clear away the remnants of last night's dinner. You don't need to begin your writing from a higher place. Start where you are.

Left to its own devices, writing is rather like the weather. It has drama, a form, a force that shapes the day. Just as good rain clears the air, good writing clears the psyche. There is something very right about just letting yourself write.

As children, words give us power, but at some stage we seem to lose out on that power. Our youngest grandson went through that delightful two-year old stage of speaking in commands: 'Stay Mammy', 'Out', 'Go', 'No' and constantly and adoringly, 'Mammy princess'. He had power over his words and we were left in no doubt as to the meaning he meant to convey.

The stage we're most likely to begin to lose out on our power over words is in school, where 'well written' and 'good grammar' are the sought-for criteria; phrases that sing off the page, innovative word combinations, paragraphs of free association and digression are frowned upon. Pedestrian prose stripped of personality and passion, perhaps elevated in tone as though writing has to be done from the loftiest of motives, is all too frequently lauded. As a result, many of us write too carefully. We try too hard. Ideally, we should give ourselves permission to hang out on the page.

So let's hang out for a while.

Get three blank A-4 pages. Begin at the top of the first, and throughout those three pages describe how and what you are feeling now, physically, emotionally and psychologically. Don't be afraid to put a label on your emotions. Write about anything and everything that crosses your mind.

This is what's called a free-form exercise. We looked at similar applications in Getting Started. You can't get it wrong. Be mean, petty, whining, scared. Be excited, sexy, adventurous, joyous. The important thing is to be whatever and however you are at this time. Get current. Most of us aren't current enough – we wonder about the future and agonise over the past. There's nothing we can do about the past – it's over, done, kaput. We can't identify what our future holds; we have no way of knowing and cannot control what happens. But we are in full control of our now and should exult in it. We will never experience these seconds, minutes, hours again.

So get down to write and allow yourself to feel the current of your own thoughts and emotions. And yes, I know – the fluidity of your thoughts can (and probably will) dry up mid-stream and every word can become a commitment, a matter for scrutiny. If that happens, ignore the sensation and keep going. Keep that hand moving and simply hang out on that page. When you've finished the three pages, stop. Put the pages away. You don't need to read them now.

WRITING TO RECORD

Recording is only taking therapy a stage further in that we record specific incidents: our first kiss, the day a child was born, the occasion we passed our driving test, the memories of the older generation.

Increasingly I come across people who want to leave a record for posterity, many for their children. A recently widowed woman who we'll call Mary, deep in the throes of mourning, came to one of my groups with only one objective in mind. She wanted to leave a record of her life and the lives of her parents and grandparents for her grandchildren.

Mary's grief was raw, but she never missed a session. She wrote within the group and at home, by hand, fluently and painfully. Instinctively, she knew that to make her recording authentic, she had to revisit sorrow as well as joy. And she did, remembering in all its poignant detail the day her best friend died in a house fire (she was twelve at the time). Mary also wrote of the deprivations of growing up in the Midlands, the economics of the times, the food the family ate, the clothes they wore. She was awed by how one memory triggered another.

Somewhere along the way, she acquired a word processor and enrolled for lessons in the local VEC. She took to the classes like the proverbial duck to water, likening processing to typing, which she had done during her stint as a receptionist in the old Jury's Hotel in Dublin's Dame Street.

That triggered her memory of the evening when poet Patrick Kavanagh came into the hotel, clutching an injured magpie under his coat. He dispatched her from her position on the front desk to the kitchen to get a saucer of milk. Tenderly he removed the magpie and, stroking its head, guided its beak towards the saucer. Unafraid, it took a few sips. Kavanagh tucked it back under his coat, raised his hat to her and the few curious guests and stepped back out into street.

She later wrote up the incident for RTÉ's 'Sunday Miscellany' slot and duly went into studio to read her piece. She insisted on framing the original cheque – she wouldn't hear of photocopying it – and admitted that she felt like a real writer, which, of course, she had been from the day she first took pen to paper to record.

There's no mystique about recording. If you haven't got a notebook to hand, when you have a quiet minute, just write down your impressions, what was said, who said what, your own thoughts. Having a sense of direction also helps. Writing is about getting something down, not about thinking something up.

When you stop writing to 'think something up', your writing becomes something that you have to stretch to achieve. It might become loftier than you are, perhaps so lofty that it moves beyond your grasp. When you're focused on getting down, say, that heady moment of having passed your driving test, you bring a sense of attention to your writing without any strain.

Mary was so focused on recall that she never had to stop to 'think something up'. Her writing, while at times grammatically incorrect and in need of rewriting and editing, sparkled with a life of its own and, very importantly, was exclusively in her own voice.

Another way to approach recording is to imagine you're taking dictation, not giving it. Listen to the voices in your head and jot down what they're telling you about whatever situation you're recording. You're transcribing, rather than generating, the flow of ideas. If you find yourself struggling, chances are it's because you're trying to speak on the page rather than listen.

Most of us are determined to write only well, and this is when the act of writing becomes a strain. We're trying to accomplish two things at one time: to communicate to people and to simultaneously impress them. Is it any wonder that our prose buckles under the strain of this double-tasking?

When we 'forget ourselves' and lose the ego, ignoring style until another day, it's much easier to write, whether it's for therapy or to record, even if it's for a first draft of a short story or a novel. By forgetting ourselves, we become a vehicle for self-expression, the storyteller, and in the process we often write very well; we certainly write more easily.

11

*awards
and
prizes*

AWARDS AND PRIZES FOR NOVELS AND BODIES OF WORK

In alphabetical order, the main awards include the following.

The Betty Trask Awards

These awards are for the benefit of young authors under the age of 35 and are given on the strength of a first novel (published or unpublished) of a romantic or traditional nature. Prizes totalling in the region of £25,000 are presented each year. The winners are required to use the money for a period or periods of foreign travel. Send SAE for entry form. Details: Awards Secretary, The Society of Authors, 84 Drayton Gardens, London SW10 9SB. Tel: 020 7373 6642; e-mail: info@societyofauthors.org; website: www.societyofauthors.org.

British Book Awards

Known as 'The Nibbies', the British Book Awards are the Oscars of the book trade. Organised by *Publishing News*, they have been an annual event since 1990. Categories include: Author of the Year, Thriller of the Year, Newcomer of the Year, Book of the Year, and of recent years, Richard and Judy's Best Read of the Year. Information from: info@midaspr.co.uk.

The CBI/Bisto Book of the Year Award

The CBI/Bisto Book of the Year Awards are one of the main annual children's book awards in Ireland. Now in their seventeenth year, they have been sponsored since their inception by Bisto (RHM Foods). The awards are made annually by Children's Books Ireland to an author or illustrator born or resident in Ireland. The shortlist is announced in April and the awards in June for books published during the previous year. There are a total of five awards: CBI/Bisto Book of the Year: €3,000, as well as a perpetual trophy and framed certificate. Three Merit Awards, shared prize fund of €3,000. The Eilis Dillon Award has a €1,000 award and trophy.

The Glen Dimplex New Writers Awards

Run in association with the Irish Writers' Centre, these awards are for emerging writers. The prize fund is €45,000. Categories include the best first book published by an author within fiction, poetry, children's literature and biography/non-fiction. A fifth category is for the best first book published in any genre in the Irish language. The GD New Writer of the Year will be chosen from the five category winners. For more, log on to www.newwritersawards.ie. For enquiries and further information, contact Grace Aungier, Awards Co-ordinator, c/o Irish Writers' Centre, 19 Parnell Square, Dublin 1.

International IMPAC Dublin Literary Award

This award is the largest of its kind. It is administered by Dublin City Public Libraries and nominations are made by libraries in capital and major cities throughout the world. Titles are nominated solely on the basis of 'high literary merit' and books may be written in any language. The prize is €100,000 if the book is written in English. If the winning book is an English translation, the author receives €75,000 and the translator €25,000. Details: tel: 01 674 4802; fax: 01 674 4879; e-mail: literaryaward@dublincity.ie; website: www.impacdublinaward.ie.

The Irish Book Awards (IBA)

Instigated by booksellers Hughes & Hughes, this is now an annual event. It comprises The Irish Novel of the Year, sponsored by Hughes & Hughes, with a prize of €10,000; Non-Fiction Book of the Year, sponsored by Argosy Book Wholesalers, which carries a prize of €7,500; and The Irish Children's Book of the Year, sponsored by The Dublin Airport Authority, with a prize of €5,000.

Irish PEN/A.T. Cross Award

This award is for a significant body of work, written and produced over a number of years by an Irish-born writer who has made an outstanding contribution to Irish literature. The award is open to novelists, playwrights, poets, scriptwriters, etc. Members of Irish PEN, as well as previous winners, nominate and vote for the candidate. In keeping with the tradition started at the W.B. Yeats dinner in 1935, the writer is presented with the award in the company of other writers at Irish PEN's annual dinner.

Listowel Writers' Week/The Kerry Group Irish Fiction Award.

A prize of €10,000 for a published work of fiction by an Irish author. Closing date beginning of March. Details from Writers' Week, 24 The Square, Listowel, Co. Kerry; tel: 068 21074; fax: 068 22893; e-mail: writersweek@eircom.net; website: www.writersweek.ie.

The Man Booker Prize

This annual prize for fiction of £65,000, including £2,500 to each of the shortlisted authors, is awarded to the best novel published each year. Entries only from UK publishers who may each submit two novels with scheduled publication dates between 1 October of the previous year and 30 September of the current year. Details: Colman Getty PR, Middlesex House, 34-42 Cleveland Street, London WIT 4JE. Tel: 020 7631 2666; fax: 020 7631 2699; e-mail: alice@colmangettypr.co.uk; website: www.themanbookerprize.co.uk. Contact: Alice Kavanagh.

The Man Booker International Prize

A prize of £60,000, awarded bi-annually to a living author published in or translated to English. This complements the annual Man Booker Prize by recognising one writer's achievement in continued creativity, development and overall contribution to fiction. Literary excellence is the prize's sole focus. Details: Colman Getty PR, Middlesex House, 34-42 Cleveland Street, London WIT 4JE. Tel: 020 7631 2666; e-mail: pr@colmangetty.co.uk; website: www.manbookerinternational.com.

Orange Prize for Fiction

An award of £30,000 and a statuette fondly known as 'The Bessie' is for a novel written in English by a woman of any nationality and first published in the UK between 1 April and 31 March. Details: Booktrust, Book House, 45 East Hill, London SW18 2QZ. Tel: 020 8516 2986; fax: 020 8516 2978; e-mail: hannah@booktrust.org.uk. Contact: Hannah Rutland.

Orange Award for New Writers

£10,000 awarded annually to an emerging female fiction-writing talent with a first work of fiction – a novel, novella or short story collection. Applications welcome from women of any age or nationality whose first work of fiction is published in book form between 1 April and 31 March each year. Details: Booktrust, Book House, 45 East Hill, London SW18 2QZ. Tel: 020 8516 2986; fax: 020 8516 2978; e-mail: hannah@booktrust.org.uk. Contact: Hannah Rutland.

The Rooney Prize for Irish Literature

An annual prize of £10,000 is awarded to encourage young Irish writing talent. To be eligible, individuals must be Irish, under 40 years of age and have published a body of work which can include a play, novel, collection of short stories or poetry. The prize is non-competitive and there is no application procedure or entry form. Details: J.A Sherwin, Strathin, Templecarrig, Delgany, Co. Wicklow. Tel: 287 4769; fax: 287 2595; e-mail: rooneyprize@ireland.com.

Whitbread Book Awards

These awards celebrate and promote contemporary writing. Writers must be resident in Great Britain or Ireland for three or more years. Judged in two stages and offering a total of £50,000 prize money, there are five categories: Novel, First Novel, Biography, Poetry and Children's. Entries are judged by a panel of three judges and the winner in each category receives £5,000. Nine judges then choose the Whitbread Book of the Year from the five category winners. The overall winner receives £25,000. Submissions must be received from publishers. Closing date: June/July. Details: Alan Stanton, The Booksellers Association, Minster House, 272 Vauxhall Bridge Road, London SW1V 1BA. Tel: 020 7802 0801; fax: 020 7802 0803; e-mail: alan.stanton@booksellers.co.uk; website: www.whitbreadbookawards.co.uk.

AWARDS AND PRIZES FOR SHORT STORIES, ESSAYS AND PLAYS

Christopher Ewart-Biggs Memorial Prize

A prize of £5,000 is awarded once every two years to the writer, of any nationality, whose work is judged to contribute most to peace and understanding in Ireland; closer ties between the people of Britain and Ireland; co-operation between the partners of the European Union. Information from The Secretary, Memorial Prize, Flat 3, 149 Hamilton Terrace, London NW8 9QS. Fax: 020 7328 0699.

The David St John Thomas Charitable Trust Competitions & Awards

A programme of writing competitions and awards totalling £20,000-£30,000. Regulars are the annual ghost story and annual love story (each 1,600-1,800 words with £1,000 as first prize). Publication of winning entry is guaranteed, usually in *Writers News/Writing Magazine* and/or an anthology. Details The David St John Thomas Charitable Trust, PO Box 6055, Nairn, IV12 4YB. Tel: 01667 453351; e-mail: dsjtcharity-nairn@fsmail.ne. Contact: Lorna Edwardson. (For full details of these and other awards, including annual writers' group anthology, send a large SAE.)

The David T.K. Wong Prize for Short Fiction

The purpose of this biennial international prize is to promote literary excellence in the form of the short story written in English. Stories must be unpublished and between 2,500 and 6,000 words. Entries must incorporate one or more of International PEN's ideals as set out in its Charter. Entries should be submitted via the entrant's local PEN Centre. The closing date for 2007/8 is end of September 2007. First prize: £7,500. Copies of PEN's Charter and addresses of PEN Centres can be found on the website of International PEN.

Details: International PEN, 9-10 Charterhouse Buildings, Goswell Road, London, ECIM 7AT. Tel: 020 7253 4308; fax: 020 7253 5711; e-mail: info@internationalpen.org.uk; website: www.internationalpen.org.uk.

E.M. Forster Award

English author E.M Forster bequeathed the American publishing rights and royalties of his posthumous novel *Maurice* to Christopher Isherwood, who transferred them to the American Academy of Arts and Letters for the establishment of an E.M. Forster Award. Currently this award is in the region of $15,000, and is given annually to a British or Irish writer for a stay in the US. Details from the American Academy of Arts and Letters, 633 West 155th Street, New York, NY 10032, USA.

Fish International Short Story Prize

An annual award, open to anyone writing in English, which aims to discover and publish new writers. Story length should be 5,000 words maximum. First prize €10,000; second one week at Anam Cara Writers' Retreat in West Cork + €250, third €250. Twelve runners-up will each receive €100. Winning stories will be published in the Fish Anthology. Entry fee: €15.00 per story. Closing date: Usually the end of November. Winners announced: 17 March. Details: Fish Publishing, Durrus, Bantry, Co Cork. Tel: 027 55645; e-mail: info@fishpublishing.com; website: www.fishpublishing.com.

Francis MacManus Short Story Competition

For more than twenty years, this competition has been run annually by RTÉ Radio 1 in memory of the late Francis MacManus, writer and broadcaster. The competition is open to people born or normally resident in Ireland. Entries should be written for radio and should be within the range of 1,900–2,000 words, i.e. a fifteen-minute slot. The prizes are

€3,000 plus a commemorative trophy for the winning story; €2,000 for second and €1,000 for third. For further information send a stamped addressed envelope to Francis MacManus Awards, RTÉ Radio Centre, Dublin 4; or log on to www.rte.ie.

The Frank O'Connor International Short Story Award

This is for a collection of short stories written by a living author, published for the first time, in English anywhere in the world, and entered by the publisher. The annual prize is €35,000. Further information: The Munster Literature Centre, Frank O'Connor House, 84 Douglas St, Cork. Website: www.munsterlit.ie.

Hennessy Award

The Hennessy Literary Awards have been in existence since 1970. Entry is through the *Sunday Tribune* which on the first Sunday of each month publishes a short story not in excess of 2,500 words and written in either English or Irish. Published pieces are eligible for the award, announced in November. Categories are: Best Emerging Fiction, Best Emerging Poetry, First Fiction. Each category winner receives a prize of €1,500, while the overall winner receives an additional €2,500 plus the trophy for Hennessy New Irish Writer. Details: Ciaran Carty, *The Sunday Tribune*, 15 Lr Baggot Street, Dublin 2. Tel: 01 661 5555.

Listowel Writers' Week

This internationally recognised festival runs several writing competitions, which include: **The Bryan MacMahon Short Story Award**. A prize of €2,500 (not more than 3,000 words). Entry fee €8.00. **Duais Foras na Gaeilge**. A prize of €1,100 for a work in Irish. Entry fee €8.00. **Eamon Keane Full-Length Play**. The winning full-length stage play receives a prize of €1,000. Entry fee €20.00. **Writers' Week Originals**

Competition. There is a prize of €650 each for Short Story (maximum 1,500 words); **Humorous Essay** (maximum 750 words); and **Short Poem.** Entry fee €8.00 with each submission. **Writing in Prisons.** A prize of €1,200 is offered for a work by a prisoner. **Irish Post/Stena Line New Writing Competition** (this competition is not open to Irish residents). The categories are Journalism and Short Story. Further details of this are advertised in the 'Irish Post' UK. Poetry Competition for which there are two prize categories. €900 for a single poem of not more than 70 lines; €900 for best collection of poems (six to twelve), as well as financial support towards publication. Entry fee: €8 with each single poem; €25.00 with each collection. **Kerry County Council Creative Writing Competitions for Youth.** There is a prize fund of €1,300 for Creative Writing for 9 years and under (maximum 300 words); Creative Writing for 12 years and under (maximum 500 words); Creative Writing for 14 years and under (maximum 500 words); Creative Writing for 16 years and under (maximum 1,000 words); Creative Writing for 18 years and under (maximum 1,000 words). A limerick for all age groups up to 18 years. Entry fee: €1.00 with each entry. Enquiries, further information and details from Writers' Week, 24 The Square, Listowel, Co Kerry, tel: 068 21074; fax: 068 22893; e-mail: writersweek@eircom.net; website: www.writersweek.ie.

The National Short Story Prize

This annual award is a collaboration between BBC Radio 4, NESTA (the National Endowment for Science, Technology and the Arts) and *Prospect* magazine. Its primary aim is to re-establish the importance of the British short story. It is funded by NESTA and administered in conjunction with Booktrust and Scottish Booktrust. The winning award is worth £15,000 – the largest first prize in the world for a single story – and there is a runner-up award of £3,000 and three further shortlisted authors will receive awards of £500 each.

The five shortlisted stories will be broadcast on Radio 4. This award is open to authors with a previous record of publication who are either UK nationals or residents. Entries may be unpublished or previously published stories. Entry form can be downloaded from www.bbc.co.uk. There are also details on how to enter, plus the terms and conditions governing the award, including the eligibility criteria.

The V.S. Pritchett Memorial Prize

An annual prize of £1,000 is awarded for a previously unpublished short story of up to 5,000 words. Entry fee: £5.00 per story. For entry forms contact the Secretary. The writer must be a citizen of the UK, Commonwealth or Ireland. Details: The Royal Society of Literature, Somerset House, The Strand, London WC2R 1LA. Tel: 020 7845 4676; fax: 020 7845 4679; e-mail: info@rslit.org; website: www.rslit.org.

In addition, there are various magazine, newspaper and association competitions for which you'll have to keep a look out – *Woman's Way*, *Ireland's Eye* and *Ireland's Own* run short story competitions regularly. There are also several smaller well-established competitions which are listed blow in alphabetical order.

Bill Naughton Short Story Competition

Information from: Bill Naughton Short Story Competition, Box No 2005, Aghamore, Ballyhaunis, Co. Mayo. Website: www.aghamoregaa.com.

Drogheda Amergin Creative Writing Awards

Started as a writing class for the unemployed, Drogheda Creative Writers evolved into a writers' group. It organises the annual Drogheda Amergin Creative Writing Awards. For information, contact Nuala Early on 041 984 2893 or www.droghedawriters.com.

Orange Northern Woman Short Story Prize

Open to local women writers. To enter, submit a fictional short story (approximately 1,250–1,500 words) to the Editor, Orange NW Short Story Prize, Greer Publications, 5b Edgewater Business Park, Belfast BT3 9JQ. For details, e-mail: lynpalmer@greerpublications.com.

Wicklow Writers

Information and entry form from: Tess Doyle, 21 Dunbar Glen, Wicklow.

Writers' & Artists' Yearbook Short Story Competition

For both published and aspiring writers. For details, terms and conditions visit www.acblack.com/shortstorycompetition.

12

grammar matters

'I will not go down to posterity talking bad grammar.'
Benjamin Disraeli

12

grammar matters

'I will not go down to posterity talking bad grammar.'
Benjamin Disraeli

WORDS

Words are a writer's basic tool. Use them carefully, sparingly and lovingly.

- Choose the words that are best for the job, that say exactly what you mean.
- Strive for brevity, clarity and vividness. Don't use 'contribute' when you mean 'give'.
- Simplify technical terms. For example, don't say 'carcinoma', say 'cancer'.
- Avoid unnecessary wordiness and use simple words where possible. Instead of 'a member of the feline species', write 'cat'.
- Be specific. It's vague to say 'a cake', but 'a chocolate cake with fudge icing' is specific.
- Avoid trite, trendy or hackneyed phrases. They're either the mark of an amateur or a sign of downright laziness. Such phrases include: at this point in time; fit as a fiddle; along the lines of; in the region of; in the pink; good as gold; nipped in the bud, etc.

SENTENCES

A sentence is a group of words that expresses at least one complete thought. This means that something definite is said. For this to happen, the group of words must contain or imply a verb.

The subject of a sentence is the person or thing who/that performs the action. The predicate is the part containing the action (not just the verb). In the sentence 'The man writes daily', *the man* is the subject and *writes daily* is the predicate.

- Don't crowd too many details into a sentence.
- Avoid repeating the same words or phrases in a sentence.
- For newspaper features, use short, snappy sentences and clear words.
- While there is more leeway for greater diversity and more complex sentence construction in magazine features and fiction, keep to the maxim of conveying exactly what you mean.
- When writing for radio, aim for precision but edit for 'radio-speak' and look for opportunities to create visual pictures.

PARAGRAPHS

The modern trend when writing paragraphs is to keep them short. When you use a short paragraph you give the reader facts and ideas in a smaller package, which is easier to handle, as the mind can grasp a small unit of thought more readily than a large one. There are two cardinal rules for paragraphs:
• They should contain related ideas.
• They should function as a unit.

Generally, tabloid newspapers use shorter paragraphs than broadsheets, though now that broadsheets are changing format to tabloid – with even the *Guardian*, regarded since the 1800s as the ultimate bastion of conservatism, adopting the 'berliner' format – perceptions are easing and bending.

There are no specific guidelines for either trade or social magazines. House style is usually followed.

Fiction and non-fiction books are dependent on individual writing style. In writing for radio, while sentences and paragraphs will not be neatly rounded off, remember that the listener's mind can grasp small units of thought more easily than large ones.

PARTS OF SPEECH

Nouns

A noun is the name of a person, place or thing. There are four types of nouns:
- A common noun is an ordinary object, e.g. computer, pencil, book.
- A proper noun is a specifically named object, like a person (John), a place (Ireland), a day (Tuesday) or a month (September). All proper nouns have capital letters.
- An abstract noun is the name of a quality or emotion, e.g. courage, cruelty, talent.
- A collective noun is a name for a group of similar objects that form a whole, e.g. a school of dolphins, a football team.

Verbs

A verb is an action word. Every sentence must contain or imply a verb. The tense of verbs changes depending on whether you are writing in the past, present or future.

Examples: She wrote the book in a year. (past)
He writes every day. (present)
I will write tomorrow. (future)

Wherever possible, use the active voice. A verb is in the active voice when the subject is the doer of the action.

Examples: The visitors were received by the writer in her office. (passive voice, weak)
The writer received the visitors in her office. (active voice, strong)

Verbs are the most powerful voice in the English language. They inject life, action and movement into your sentence.

Correctly chosen verbs will often dispense with the need to use an adverb.

Examples: The man walks.
The man strolls.
The man strides.

Adverbs

An adverb tells more about the action of the verb. For example, in the sentence 'I will write regularly', 'regularly' is the adverb.

Prepositions

A preposition joins a noun or pronoun to the remainder of the sentence.

Examples: She writes in biro. He writes on screen.

In the above examples, 'in' and 'on' are prepositions.

Conjunctions

Conjunctions are words or phrases that join together two parts of a sentence. Some of the most frequently used conjunctions include 'and', 'but', 'because,' 'until', 'therefore' and 'although'.

Example: I research and write because I enjoy it.

In the above example, 'because' is the conjunction. (Note: In this particular case, 'and' is merely joining two words.)

PUNCTUATION

If texting sounded the death knell to punctuation, Lynne Truss's *Eats, Shoots & Leaves* has gone a long way to dragging the subject back into popularity, giving it a trendy facelift.

Apostrophes

Apostrophes are all too frequently misused. Their inaccurate usage is one of the bugbears of grammarians. One of their correct applications is to show that something or someone owns another thing.

Examples: Mary's dictionary (the dictionary belonging to Mary)
The printer's speed (the speed of the printer)

If more than one person or thing owns another thing, the apostrophe comes after the 's'.

Example: Sean and John share a word processor. It is the boys' means of writing.

Also: when a word or two words are shortened, an apostrophe is used instead of the missing letters.

Examples: I do not = I don't
They are = they're

The mistake that is regularly made is with it is/its.

Example: It is a sunny day
can be correctly be written as
It's a sunny day.

The one and only exception is the possessive 'its'.

Example: The dog ate its dinner. (Note: The dog did not eat 'it is' dinner. 'Its' *should not* be written 'it's'.)

Capital Letters

Capital letters are used:
- At the beginning of a sentence.
- For the names of people and places, e.g. Mary, Dublin.
- In book and movie titles, e.g. *Pride and Prejudice*; *Casablanca*.
- For days and months, e.g. Tuesday, January.
- For brand names, e.g. Nike, Guinness.

Quotation Marks

Quotation marks are used when writing down precisely what someone said. In dialogue, single quotation marks (') have largely taken over from double (""), with double being used for a quote within a quotation or when a title that would usually appear in single quotes appears within a quotation.

Examples: 'Have you seen the new production of "A View from the Bridge" yet?' asked Mark.

'Writing is not a profession but a vocation of unhappiness' is a statement regularly made by writer Georges Simenon, who, for the record, also described writing as 'hell'.

A note here on dialogue: when a new character speaks, always begin on a new line.

COMMON PROBLEMS

'Affect' vs. 'Effect'

'Affect' is mostly used as a verb and 'effect' as a noun. The usual meaning of 'affect' as a verb is to 'bring about a change', as in 'her novel affected me greatly', though the verb does have a few other meanings, such as 'pretend to feel': 'she affected indifference to his story'.

The usual meaning of 'effect' as a verb is 'to bring about': 'How shall we effect a solution?'

The everyday use of 'effect' is as a noun, meaning result, as in 'the effect of editing that manuscript was remarkable', or influence: 'he has a good effect on her'.

'Due To' and 'Owing To'

If you don't know the finer point of the difference between them, you'll never go wrong with the following rule: '*due to* means caused by, *owing to* means because of'.

Gender of Pronouns

A long-standing controversy exists about the appropriate pronouns to use in sentences where such words as anyone, everybody and someone are the subject: 'Anyone can do what … want/s.'

The pronoun 'he' used in a generic way is traditional but can cause criticism for its male bias. However, 'she' is decidedly odd, though worse was the short-lived s/he. Despite not being grammatically correct, 'they' is now commonly employed.

None

The word 'none' is another target of purist criticism. Depending on sentence construction, it can be found with either a singular or a plural verb. When it precedes or refers back to a singular noun, the verb should also be in the singular: 'None of that wordage is correct.' A singular verb is also used when one can be interpreted as 'not one' or 'no one': 'None of us was aware of the problem.'

A plural verb is used when none means 'not any of a group of persons or things'.

Split Infinitive

Strong criticism has been levelled by grammatical purists at anything coming between 'to' and the verb. Today this is regarded as a cramping rule, increasing the difficulty of writing clearly and causing ambiguity in many cases. The cult TV programme *Star Trek*'s signature opening, 'To boldly go where no man has gone before' would be more grammatically correct as, 'To go boldly…'.

That and Which

All too frequently when used as relative pronouns introducing clauses, 'that' and 'which' are regarded as interchangeable. Strictly speaking 'that' should be used to indicate defining clauses, and 'which' to introduce non-defining clauses. A defining clause is one that is essential to the sense of the sentence, e.g.: 'The book that told the story of Beethoven's childhood was well researched.' Here Beethoven's childhood is a defining characteristic. A non-defining clause is one that can be regarded as a parenthesis, or digression, e.g.: 'The book, which told the story of Beethoven's childhood, was well researched.' 'Which told the story of Beethoven's childhood' is not related to the main point of the sentence and could be deleted.

Though and Although

'Though' and 'although' are exchangeable, with 'though' being the most colloquial form: 'I went to the book launch (al)though I wasn't feeling well.'

FIGURES OF SPEECH

The English language has in the region of fifty different figures of speech. The most frequently used and referred to are listed below in alphabetical order.

Figures of speech use words in a non-literal way to achieve an effect beyond the range of ordinary language. Less is more here, and used sparingly, figures of speech enrich and enhance our writing.

Alliteration

The repetition of the same consonant sounds or of different vowel sounds at the beginning of words or in stressed syllables.

Examples: 'On scrolls of silver snowy sentences.'
(repeated 's' sound)
'The soldier told a tale of trouble and torture.' (repeated 't' sound)

Anaphora

The deliberate repetition of a word or phrase at the beginning of several successive verses, clauses or paragraphs.

Example: 'We shall fight on the beaches, we shall fight on the landing grounds, we shall fight in the fields and in the streets, we shall fight in the hills.'

Assonance

Resemblance of sound, especially of the vowel sounds in words.

Example: 'That dolphin-torn, that gong-tormented sea.'

Euphemism

The act or an example of substituting a mild, indirect or vague term for one considered harsh, blunt or offensive.

Example: Using the term 'passed over' for death.

Hyperbole

An exaggerated statement used for effect and not meant to be taken literally.

Examples: I could sleep for a month.
            I had to wait an eternity for the file to download.

Irony

The use of words to express something different from, and often opposite to, their literal meaning.

Examples: Watching it rain, he said, 'Lovely day for a picnic.'
            Looking at the smashed hulk of the car, he said,
            'I finally got rid of that squeak in the dashboard.'

Malapropism

Ludicrous misuse of a word, especially by confusion with one with a similar sound.

Example: She has extra-century perception.

Metaphor

A comparison in which one thing is said to be another.

Examples: The cat's eyes were jewels.
            A sea of troubles.

Oxymoron

A rhetorical figure in which incongruous or contradictory terms are combined.

Examples: A *terrible beauty*.
            He tried to *act naturally*, but in these *plastic glasses* and *designer jeans* he looked *seriously funny*.

Onomatopoeia

The sound of words or phrases that imitate the original sound.

Examples: The burning wood *crackled* and *hissed*.

Personification

The representation of an object or concept as though it were a person.

Examples: Time stood still.
Love enfolded us in her arms.
Foolishness walks in the crowd.

Simile

A figure of speech in which two essentially unlike things are compared, often introduced by *like* or *as*.

Examples: 'My love is like a red, red rose.'
The mob surged forward like a burst dam.
Fresh as a daisy.

Tmesis

The separation of the parts of a compound word, usually to create a humorous effect. A modern ploy.

Examples: Abso-bloody-lutely.
Fan-f***ing-tastic.

Understatement

Restraint or lack of emphasis in expression.

Example: 'I think we've a bit of trouble here,' said John as his printer groaned to a halt.

13

addenda

'Writers seldom wish other writers well.' Saul Bellow

READING GROUPS

Francis Bacon wasn't wrong when he said 'Reading maketh a full man'. The majority of us writers are voracious readers, though invariably we read alone and in private, devouring the latest books that tickle our fancy. We're often thrown into despair at a brilliantly written book, and equally have our confidence boosted after reading a not-so-good book – after all, it did get published.

When we read well-written material, it imbues in us style, graceful narration, plot development and the creation of believable characters. Being held in utter enthrallment by a combination of a great story and great writing is part of every writer's necessary formation. You are unlikely to sweep someone away by the force of your writing unless you yourself have been swept away.

The general consensus is that it's difficult to write material which will be suitable for publication if you don't read. By reading we experience the mediocre and the downright awful. Such experiences help us to recognise these traits when they creep into our own writing. We also read to measure ourselves against the good and the great, to experience different styles of writing and to gain a sense of what can be achieved with words.

If you remember, Anne Enright's advice is read, read, read. For those interested in reading, look into www.lovereading.co.uk. This UK website, which is free, allows you to download and print opening extracts of books, with a 'like-for-like' author recommendation service. You can also receive regular e-mail updates of new books in your favourite genres.

Also keep an eye out for World Book Day (www.world-bookday.com) held in March. This is the biggest annual event supporting books and reading in the UK and Ireland, with schools, libraries, bookshops and other venues participating.

For a writer, one of the most important aspects of reading is that it creates an ease and intimacy with the process of writing. Constant reading helps bring you to a place where you can write eagerly and without self-consciousness. It also provides a constantly growing knowledge of what has been done and what hasn't, what's trite and what's fresh, what works and what lies dead on the page. Stephen King maintains, 'The more you read, the less apt you are to make a fool of yourself with your pen or word processor.'

If you're looking for company and discussion around your reading, there's no better solution than to join a reading group. Such is the popularity of this growth area that in the UK, family reading groups have been set up. Shortly after its inception at the end of 2005, several hundred readers had signed up to *The Telegraph*'s Family Book Club, where parents and children meet to discuss a chosen book. It's no surprise that the first month's choice was C S. Lewis's *The Lion, the Witch and the Wardrobe*.

Reading groups are recognised by publishers as playing an increasingly important – albeit subconscious – role in the marketing of books. Oftentimes a book that hasn't been particularly strongly promoted by the publishers will be picked up by a group, and by word of mouth will become known and a popular read. In the trade these are known as 'whisper' books. Probably one of the best known 'whisper' titles of recent times is *The Kite Runner*, the debut novel of Khaled Hosseini. Described as an epic story of fathers and sons, friendship and betrayal, it runs from the final days of Afghanistan's monarchy to the atrocities of the present. It was an unlikely international bestseller.

In the UK, the book club slot in Channel 4's *Richard and Judy Show* has given popular fiction an enormous boost, as have the regular author slots on TV3's *Ireland AM*. Previously, reading groups in Ireland had received an unknown prominence courtesy of broadcaster Marian Finucane's morning radio show on RTÉ Radio 1. Since the 9.00 to 10.00 morning slot has been taken over by Ryan Tubridy, book clubs have received a further shot in the arm with the advent of the Barry's Tea Book Club. Check it out on www.barrystea.ie/bookclub.

Libraries in both Northern and Southern Ireland have also copped on to the importance of reading groups. Northern Ireland Libraries (www.ni-libraries.net) has reading groups for adults, teenagers and pre-teens based in several local libraries.

Dublin City Libraries (www.dublincity.ie/living-in-the-city/libraries) run a series of Readers' Days for both adults and children in various civic offices for members and reading groups where books and reading are celebrated; selected authors talk about their books, writing and influences; and discussions are held.

WRITING GROUPS

At last count, throughout Ireland there were more than 100 writing groups. If you're interested, check with The Irish Writers' Union and local libraries to find one in your area. Some meet weekly, others fortnightly, mostly during the winter months, others are in contact all year round.

Writing is a lonely business and the companionship and support of a group of like-minded people with the same interest and on the same wavelength can be of enormous benefit.

Some professional writers have formed their own groups, which meet regularly and have the ability to be constructively analytical about each other's work. Such groups are closed shops to unpublished, unproven writers.

Writers who have not yet been published should be aware that assessment of work earmarked for publication is better carried out by an outside professional rather than at group level, because let's face it, the majority of people in writing groups haven't yet been published, don't know the publishing business and have no idea of market demands or even how to bring a manuscript up to a publishable level. The majority of participants in writing groups produce first drafts of varying standards, which is why the most vibrant writing groups employ regular guest speakers, some of whom will have a brief of analysing and advising on work in progress.

addenda

PROFESSIONAL COURSES

While courses on writing are an invaluable tool for the aspiring writer, it's important to practise and develop your own creative skills. Not for nothing is writing dubbed the lonely profession. While you can get help in various areas, nobody can find ideas for you, write for you, do your research, carry out a preliminary edit or suss out the market. That's all up to you.

You wouldn't plan to practise as an architect without studying to acquire the relevant knowledge or aim to become a professional footballer without training and honing your techniques. The same degree of dedication applies to writing.

Courses for writers are on a constant growth curve. 'The last few years have seen an increase in the number and variety of writing courses on offer by the UCD Adult Education Centre. There has been a significant increase in interest and participation in our writing courses,' says director of UCD Adult Education Centre, Bairbre Fleming.

Listed below are just some of the outlets where writing courses are taught by professionals:
- Irish Writers Centre, Dublin (www.writerscentre.ie).
- Listowel Writers' Week (www.writersweek.ie).
- Trinity College Dublin (TCD) (www.tcd.ie/owc/courses/creative).
- Queen's University, Belfast (www.qub.ac.uk).
- University College Dublin (UCD) Adult Education Programme (www.ucd.ie/adulted).

All kinds of creative writing courses, both virtual and real, can be checked out by doing a search on the internet. In addition, keep an eye on the notice board in your local library, in the 'what's on' columns of newspapers and notices in your locality.

RETREATS

These are some of the residential getaways where writers, and indeed, in many cases, other artists, are encouraged to hone their craft in the company of other like-minded people while being physically and mentally nurtured.

Allihies Language and Arts Centre, Beara Penninsula, Co. Cork. E-mail: allihies-language@netcourrier.com; website: www.allihies.ie. Director: Dave Caffrey. The centre is for professors in the liberal arts and their students on study abroad programmes. It's suitable for hosting seminars and workshops in literary studies and the arts for groups of 20-30 participants and their instructors. The centre also organises independent creative workshops in various disciplines for individual participants. See the events link on the website for details.

Anam Cara Writers' and Artists' Retreat, Eyeries, Beara, Co. Cork. Tel: 027 74441; fax: 027 74448; e-mail: anamcararetreat@eircom.net; website:www.anamcararetreat.com. Director: Sue Booth-Forbes. For novices as well as experienced writers and artists, the retreat provides comfort and support for creative people to focus on their own projects. The centre also offers specially tailored workshops throughout the year.

Tyrone Guthrie Centre, Annaghmakerrig, Newbliss, Co. Monaghan. Tel: 047 54003; fax: 047 54380; e-mail: info@tyroneguthrie.ie; website: www.tyroneguthrie.ie. The late Tyrone Guthrie's home is a workplace for writers, artists, sculptors and musicians. It receives financial support from both An Chomhairle Ealaíon (The Irish Arts Council) and the Arts Council of Northern Ireland. The main accommodation houses up to eleven artists, with self-catering farmyard cottages available for a further six. Details of facilities, cost and bursaries, as well as an application form, are on the website.

addenda

SOCIETIES AND ASSOCIATIONS

Irish PEN, tel: 01 296 4679; e-mail: irishpen@ireland.com; website: www.irishpen.com. Irish PEN, which is affiliated to International PEN, is an association of both established and new writers. Over the years, Irish PEN has campaigned and lobbied on subjects such as censorship, the imposition of VAT on books, retention of Section 481 to safeguard Ireland's film industry and for the retention of the Writers and Artists Tax Exemption Scheme. Monthly meetings with guest speakers are held at The United Arts Club in Dublin. Each year at the Annual Dinner the Irish PEN/AT Cross Award is presented to an Irish-born writer who has made an outstanding contribution to Irish literature.

Irish Writers' Union, 19 Parnell Square, Dublin 1. Tel: 01 872 1302; e-mail: iwu@ireland-writers.com; website: www.ireland-writers.com. The IWU has represented Irish writers in their professional dealings with publishers and government since 1987. It has campaigned against abolition of writers' tax exemption and for introduction of PLR so writers would be paid for borrowings of their books from libraries.

LITERARY FESTIVALS

Cúirt International Festival of Literature, Galway, has been going strong for more than twenty years. It is usually held in the spring and is a festival of literary delights with international authors reading alongside Irish writers. Contact Maura Kennedy, Programme Director, Cúirt International Festival of Literature, Galway Arts Centre, 47 Dominick Street, Galway. Tel: 091 565 886; e-mail: maura@galwayartscentre.ie.

Dublin Writers' Festival, held at various locations around Dublin in mid-June to take in Bloomsday on the 16th. Programme includes readings, discussions, public interviews and other events of literary interest, involving approximately forty Irish and international poets and fiction writers. Details on www.dublinwritersfestival.com.

Edgeworth Literary Festival has taken place in the spring for the past ten years and includes workshops and competitions. Details from www.edgeworthliteraryfestival.com.

Franco-Irish Literary Festival is held in Dublin Castle's Coach House and Chester Beatty Library in early summer. Its aim is to widen and enhance the relationship between Ireland and France. French, Irish and European writers take part in discussions, interviews and readings. Further information is available at www.francoirishliteraryfestival.com.

IMRAM, the Irish Literary Festival in Derry in association with Bláthanna Festival, is a springtime week-long celebration of readings, music and concerts.

International Poetry Festival, Dun Laoghaire, Co. Dublin. Details are available from www.dlrcoco.ie/arts/festival.html.

Listowel Writers' Week, usually held the last weekend in May. Now in its 36th year, it's a colourful festival of writing, drama, cinema as well as an extensive art programme. The centrepiece of the festival is the writing workshops to suit different levels and interests. Further information is available at www.writersweek.ie.

addenda

USEFUL CONTACTS AND INFORMATION

Arts Council, The, 70 Merrion Square, Dublin 2. Tel: 01 618 0200; website: www.artscouncil.ie. The Arts Council exists to stimulate public interest and to promote the knowledge, appreciation and practice of the arts.

Aosdána (www.artscouncil.ie/aosdana) was established by The Arts Council to honour artists whose work has made an outstanding contribution to the arts in Ireland.

Arts Council of Northern Ireland, MacNeice House, 77 Malone Road, Belfast, BT9 6AQ. Tel: 028 9038 5200; e-mail: info@artscouncil-ni.org; website: www.artscouncil-ni.org. Provides support for artists and arts organisations in Northern Ireland.

Askaboutwriting.net, e-mail: news@askaboutwriting.net; website: www.askaboutwriting.net. An Internet resource site which publishes general writing news and news of events, competitions and what's on where. It updates on Saturdays and is e-mailed on Mondays to a permission-based list to which anybody is welcome to subscribe. While the focus is on Irish and UK opportunities, the site has an international readership with ex-pats regularly logging on for home news.

The Author, 84 Drayton Gardens, London SW10 9SB. Tel: 020 7373 6642, Quarterly, £12. This magazine, the organ of the Society of Authors, is a mine of information and was founded in 1890.

Carousel – The Guide to Children's Books, The Saturn Centre, 54-76 Bissell Street, Birmingham, B5 7HX. Tel: 0121 622 7458; fax: 0121 666 7526; e-mail: carousel.guide@virgin.net; website: www.carousel.guide.co.uk. Three issues per annum, £10.50. Reviews fiction, non-fiction and poetry for children, plus articles and author profiles. Founded 1995.

Children's Books Ireland (CBI), 17 North Great George's Street, Dublin 1. Tel: 01 872 7475; website: www.childrensbooksireland.com. Is a resource and advocacy organisation for adults which provides leadership and support in the promotion and celebration of books and reading for children throughout Ireland. (Book Trust is CBI's UK equivalent.) CBI activities include *Inis* magazine, The CBI/Bisto Book of the Year Awards, Annual Summer School and The Children's Book Festival.

CLÉ – The Irish Book Publishers' Association, 25 Denzille Lane, Dublin 2. Tel: 01 639 4868; e-mail: info@publishingireland.com; website: www.publishingireland.com. President: Fergal Tobin, administrator: Jolly Ronan. CLÉ is a cross-border organisation founded in 1970 so that publishers could share expertise and resources.

Freelance Market News, Sevendale House, 7 Dale Street, Manchester, M1 1 JB. Tel: 0161 228 2362, ext. 210; fax: 0161 228 3533; e-mail: fmn@writersbureau.com; website: www.writersbureau.com. Information on UK and overseas publications with editorial content, submission requirements and contact details. News of editorial requirements for writers. Features on the craft of writing, competitions, etc. Founded 1968. An open-access website is maintained. Posted are a sample contract and a FAQ on potential problems and pitfalls. Full membership is open to writers who have published or self-published at least one book. Associate membership is available to writers who are actively writing but not yet published.

National Union of Journalists (NUJ), 2nd Floor, Spencer House, Spencer Row, off Store Street, Dublin 1. Tel: 01 817 0340; fax: 01 817 0359; e-mail: liberty.hall@nuj.ie. Irish branch affiliated with London. Over 35,000 members worldwide, covering a range of editorial work – staff and freelance, writers and reporters, editors and sub-editors, photographers and illustrators – working in broadcasting, newspapers, magazines, books, on the internet and in public relations. Founded in 1907, the NUJ fights for journalists, their pay and conditions, their working rights and professional freedom.

BIBLIOGRAPHY

Blake, Carole, *From Pitch to Publication*, London: Macmillan, 1999.

Boran, Pat, *The Portable Creative Writing Workshop*, Dublin: New Island, 2005.

Cameron, Julia, *The Right to Write*, London: Pan Books, 2000.

Dorher, Jane, *The Internet: A Writer's Guide*, London: A&C Black (Publishers) Limited, 2004.

Kaplan, David Michael, *Rewriting*, London: A&C Black (Publishers) Limited, 1998.

King, Stephen, *On Writing*, London: Hodder & Stoughton, 2000.

McCuaig, Teresa, *Successful Writing*, London: Need2Know, 1996.

Pratchett, Terry (ed.), *Writers' & Artists' Yearbook 2006*, London: A&C Black (Publishers) Limited, 2006.

Turner, Barry (ed.), *The Writer's Handbook 2006*, London: Macmillan, 2006.

Truss, Lynne, *Eats, Shoots & Leaves*, London: Profile Books, 2003.

Wells, Gordon, *The Craft of Writing Articles*, London: Allison & Busby Ltd, 1996.

Invaluable websites:

www.amazon.co.uk
For a variety of books, great for buying reference books dealing with different aspects of writing.

www.answers.com
Online dictionary, encyclopaedia and much more, a veritable one-stop reference tool.

www.bbc.co.uk/worldservice/arts/features/howtowrite
Part of the BBC's website which includes information from professional writers on novels, radio plays, memoirs, even screen plays.

www.serve.com/hecht/words
Hecht's Web Site – wonderful words

www.rte.ie/drama
The part of RTÉ's website which gives information on plays, short stories, documentaries, etc.

www.spellingpolice.com.
The ultimate spell check

www.wikipedia.org.
The largest multilingual encyclopedia on the internet.

INDEX

A

adult education courses 127
agents 131-43
  list of 138-9
  in UK 134-6
agreement *see* contract
Allegiance 118, 151
Allen, Darina 122
Amsterdam 81
Angela's Ashes 130
Archer, Jeffrey 13
autobiography 129-30
awards and prizes 59, 62, 81, 117, 130, 181-93
  for novels and bodies of work 183-7
  for short stories, essays and plays 188-93

B

Banville, John 83
Baudelaire 1
BBC 59, 62, 69, 70, 127
Beckett, Samuel 71
Being Jordan 129
Belfast Telegraph 38, 39, 41
Bellow, Saul 208
bibliography 221
Binchy, Maeve 19, 73, 81, 95
biography 129-30
Blackstaff Press 140
book market 82-4, 124
  and marketable books 122-3
Bradby, Tom 95
Bristow, Jenny 122
Brookner, Anita 82-3
Brown, Dan 83
Browne, Vincent 40

C

Carson, Paul 81
Carty, Ciaran 71
Chang, Jung 129
Channel 4 212
Chekhov, Anton 76, 175
children's books 107-13, 140
Chronicles of Narnia, The 10
Clifford, Jonathon 152
Colette 104
commissions 33-6
Commitments, The 151
Connolly, John 19, 82
Considine, June 101
Constantine, Susannah 123
contact book 171
contacts and information 219-20
contracts 33, 144-9
cookbooks 122
copyright 34, 144-5
Cornwell, Patricia 81, 97
creativity, releasing 9-11
  see also ideas
Curious Incident of the Dog in the Nighttime, The 109
Currie, Edwina 83

D

Da Vinci Code, The 83
Daily Telegraph, The 58
Davies, Hunter 129
Deane, Seamus 11
Deceptions 101
Dickinson, Emily 131
diet books 123
directories 163
Diviners, The 97
Doyle, Roddy 5-6, 89, 96, 98, 101-2, 104, 151

Tolstoy 104
topicality 120
Trevor, William 96
Truss, Lynne 127
Tubridy, Ryan 213
TV3 212

U

Ultramarathon Man: Confessions of an All-Night Runner 120
Ulysses 9

V

Vernon God Little 81

W

Walker, Gail 39
War and Peace 104
Waterhouse, Keith 23
Waterstones 109
Wayman, Sheila 39
websites 163
    list of 221-2
What Not to Wear 123
Wild Swans 129
Wogan, Terry 58
Woman who Walked into Doors, The 89, 101-2
Woman's Way 29, 78
Woodall, Trinny 123
words 197
World Book Day 211
Writers' & Artists' Yearbook 124, 136, 193
Writers' Handbook 124, 136
writing
    ABCs of 19-20
    courses 215
    enjoyment of 72
    getting down to it 12-14
    groups 214

requirements 4-6
for therapy 175-7
to record 178-80
and would-be writers 7-8

Z

Zafón, Carlos Ruiz 101, 102